Why Justice in Innovation and Development Matters

This book argues that justice needs to be imbedded in innovation and development, both so that the fruits of technologies are distributed fairly and to ensure that social relations in the process of generation and application of new knowledge are equalised.

Drawing together updated and new writings, in this book Theo Papaioannou puts forward a relational egalitarian theory on justice in innovation and development. Papaioannou argues that it is important to ensure not only that the benefits of new technological products and services are shared equally across society but even more importantly that some level of equal social relations is required for the effective generation and application of new knowledge. By mitigating or eliminating relations of domination and oppression within innovation and ensuring equal relations between innovators, regulators, and publics, we can create an innovative and developmental society of equals.

The original relational perspective outlined in this book will be important for researchers across the fields of innovation studies, development studies, politics, and philosophy.

Theo Papaioannou is Professor of Politics, Innovation, and Development at the Open University, UK. He is also Co-Director of the Innogen Institute for Innovation Generation (Open University and University of Edinburgh) and holds visiting academic positions at various institutions, including CIMR Birkbeck College, University of London, University of Edinburgh, and University of Brighton.

Routledge Studies in Development and Society

The Prior Consultation of Indigenous Peoples in Latin America
Inside the Implementation Gap
Edited by Claire Wright and Alexandra Tomaselli

Transnational Social Mobilisation and Minority Rights
Identity, Advocacy and Norms
Corinne Lennox

Women's Economic Empowerment
Insights from Africa and South Asia
Edited by Kate Grantham, Gillian Dowie, and Arjan de Haan

Social Innovations in Post-Soviet Countries
Bakhrom Radjabov

Children, Youth and Participatory Arts for Peacebuilding
Lessons from Kyrgyzstan, Rwanda, Indonesia and Nepal
Edited by Ananda Breed, Helena-Ulrike Marambio, Kirrily Pells and Rajib Timalsina

Why Justice in Innovation and Development Matters
A Relational Egalitarian Perspective
Theo Papaioannou

For more information about this series, please visit: www.routledge.com/Routledge-Studies-in-Development-and-Society/book-series/SE0317

Why Justice in Innovation and Development Matters

A Relational Egalitarian Perspective

Theo Papaioannou

Routledge
Taylor & Francis Group
LONDON AND NEW YORK

First published 2026
by Routledge
4 Park Square, Milton Park, Abingdon, Oxon OX14 4RN

and by Routledge
605 Third Avenue, New York, NY 10158

Routledge is an imprint of the Taylor & Francis Group, an informa business

British Library Cataloguing-in-Publication Data
A catalogue record for this book is available from the British Library

ISBN: 978-1-041-09846-1 (hbk)
ISBN: 978-1-041-09847-8 (pbk)
ISBN: 978-1-003-65208-3 (ebk)

DOI: 10.4324/9781003652083

Typeset in Times New Roman
by Newgen Publishing UK

For my beloved parents, Dimitra and Dimitrios. None of my academic work would be possible without their encouragement and support over the years.

Contents

Preface

Work in academia often means publishing ideas, normative positions, and empirical research findings in different forms and at various platforms, including articles at peer-reviewed journals and working papers. One way to integrate some of these different publications and thereby address the issue of fragmentation in producing theory is to rework them into a book that puts forward a coherent argument. In what follows, I endeavour to do exactly that. I present an argument about the idea of justice in innovation and development, and I explain why it matters. However, my argument took different forms over the years. It first appeared in my 2021 open access article 'The Idea of Justice in Innovation: Applying Non-Ideal Political Theory to Address Questions of Sustainable Public Policy in Emerging Technologies' (*Sustainability*, Vol.13, No.5, article no. 2655). This was followed by other publications on the topic (see Introduction). Several chapters of the book at hand draw on these fragmented materials to put forward a more comprehensive outline of a theory of justice in innovation and development.

I found the process of putting these materials together challenging. This is for various reasons. First, some arguments were written several years back, and some others were written very recently. In between publications, my ideas have not remained the same. Rather, they have been shaped by various critical accounts of innovation and evolved through my participation in relevant debates and interactions with fellow innovation scholars and political theorists. Second, the decision about what to include and what to exclude from previously published materials was not straightforward. Some arguments had been developed as critiques of specific innovation and development theories and therefore they would have to be reworked for achieving coherence. Other arguments had been put forward in defence of a specific perspective of justice and therefore they would have to be broadened to include innovation and development. Third, reworking and updating previous publications for a book requires further research in normative thinking about innovation and development.

In this endeavour, I was not alone. A lot of people have contributed ideas and thoughts in different ways, intentionally and even unintentionally. First, I would like to acknowledge the generous interactions with colleagues at the Innogen Institute (Open University and University of Edinburgh) that I was honoured to direct for over six years, from 2018 to 2024. My position on the main stakeholders of innovation and development, namely innovators, regulators, and publics, draws on many years of research within Innogen. My participation in numerous events organised in the intellectual context of Innogen helped me to clarify ideas or indeed, to put them in order. Joyce Tait, David Wield, Joanna Chataway, Geoff Banda, Maureen Mackintosh, and many others have often played the role of a critical friend, enabling me to think in rather non-ideal or pragmatic terms about innovation and development. I would also like to acknowledge and thank Smita Srinivas who is one of those distinct scholars, debating both normative and empirical aspects of innovation and development. Her work on institutional variety and industrial policy over the years has been very influential. More importantly, her critical arguments around the neo-Schumpeterian school of economics and the role of the state in innovation have been important sources of ideas for me. I should not forget the contribution of Rafael Ziegler and Lukas Fuchs who in 2023 organised a workshop on 'Critiquing the Direction for Innovation: The Role of Justice and Exnovation' and subsequently edited a special issue of the *Journal of Responsible Innovation* on the same topic. My contribution to this workshop and the subsequent special issue, originally published as 'Directing Innovation Towards Just Outcomes: The Role of Principles and Politics', has been now revised and included in this book as Chapter 5. My conversations with Ville Takala on the relationship between innovation state and welfare state have also unlocked new paths of theoretical and empirical inquiry. Long discussions with Yeoryios Stamboulis and Thanos Fragandreas on the importance of critical innovation studies for unpacking moral and political aspects of emerging technologies have encouraged me to think hard of the approach I take in this small book.

Facilitating a normative turn in innovation and development studies and focusing on justice implications of technical and technological change presupposes a critical stand vis-à-vis the accepted wisdom of Schumpeterian and neo-Schumpeterian approaches to innovation and development. This is not because these approaches are irrelevant or redundant. Rather, it is because they can be complemented or even enhanced by emphasising also on the importance of evaluation of innovation and development from moral and political perspectives. Taking a critical stance towards theory is a methodological and epistemological choice that I often discuss with Alex Koutsogiannis. As a critical theorist himself, he keeps reminding me of the importance of interrogating normativity in politics of innovation and development. I am very much indebted for his generosity in terms of sharing new ideas and arguments. Last, but not least, my life companion Barbara Suarez and our son Dimitri Alexander should be also acknowledged for making my writing experience less isolated and more enjoyable.

Introduction

Justice has preoccupied political theorists for a long time. From Plato to Locke, Hume, and J. S. Mill all the way to Rawls, Young, and Sen, the idea of justice has been defined as a moral and political standard of how people ought to live and relate to one another within a framework of fair institutions. The fundamental requirement of social justice is to have equal regard for persons independently of their colour, gender, economic, and social background. Yet this kind of normative standard only lately entered the vocabulary of innovation and development studies, and it did so indirectly under the banners of inclusive or responsible innovation. The latter have influenced development and practice with donors promoting the view that problems such as poverty and inequality could be resolved through more inclusive or responsible innovation. Although principles of justice and related theories have been applied to govern various social and political actions, technological innovation especially remains a difficult area for the application of social justice. This is not only because of complexity of old and new technologies and their unpredictable impact on social relations and institutions but also because of epistemological perceptions of value neutrality in the innovation and development process. Papaioannou and Srinivas (2019) have paid closer attention to such perceptions, analysing the relationship between technological change and values. They have argued that innovation as such has been traditionally viewed as a process that involves techno-scientific decisions about products and services which provide solutions to problems on the ground and have nothing to do with non-epistemic or non-scientific values, e.g., ethical and political values. In this perception, such (non-scientific) values become relevant only in the stage

DOI: 10.4324/9781003652083-1

of use of technological products and services. Therefore, if a technological product such as ChatGPT is being used unethically, threatening human rights and values of freedom and equality, then it can invite criticism and potentially lose its legitimacy.

This small book starts off with the premise that innovation and development are above all human actions; as such, they are intentional and guided not only by epistemic norms (e.g. coherence, simplicity, truth, etc.) and economic values and individual interests (e.g. use/exchange values, utility, materialism, cost/profit, etc.) but also by moral and political values and social interests (e.g. freedom, equality, happiness, etc.). Indeed, the importance of the latter set of values is recognised by an increasing number of scholars (e.g. Morgan, 2015; Caldas et al, 2006; Gigerenzer and Selten, 2001) who point out the non-technical and non-economic aspects of new technologies. Innovation studies has always had traditions that well acknowledge that there is no such thing as pure innovative and/or calculative behaviour. Indeed, innovation is closely tied to values other than epistemic norms and economic values; neither markets nor innovation systems evolve spontaneously as value-free or neutral mechanisms within societies. Rather they are historical and political developments (Block, 2018; Block and Keller, 2011) which involve value judgements. As Freeman et al (1971) argued several decades ago, scientists and innovators often take refuge in neutrality of science-driven innovation, but the fact is that they remain vulnerable to the criticism of science and technology as forces pre-emptying the political making process. Markets and innovation systems can be (and ought to be) politically controlled. They can be politically directed towards delivering either morally justified benefits for society or morally unjustified costs for society.

As a value-laden human action, innovation is significant for social justice. As Buchanan et al (2011) point out, innovation creates opportunities for promoting justice but also poses risks of injustice, i.e., it can worsen existing injustice, or it can create new injustice. However, innovation as such is not a mere instrument of justice. Rather it presupposes justice to be legitimised. This book brings together some old and some new writings of mine to explain why justice in innovation and development matters. It argues that social justice is a non-ideal standard which is significant for the success and acceptance of technologies which impact on development. These technologies range from grassroots products which address basic needs of individuals, households and communities to high tech solutions for states and governments. By using the term 'non-ideal', I emphasise the importance of 'non-abstract' or 'concrete' theorising of justice in innovation. For example, when non-ideal principles of equity, recognition, and participation (Papaioannou, 2018) are embedded in emerging innovations, different publics tend to support their consolidation and scaling up for the sake of public good (Papaioannou, 2018). Therefore, these innovations succeed in achieving legitimacy for changing technological and social paradigms.

In this book, I insist that the idea of justice in innovation and development is not merely about distributing fairly the fruits of technologies but also about equalising relations in the process of generation and application of new knowledge. This is why it matters. When it comes to innovation and development, we have reasons to ensure not only the equal share of new products and services for each member of society but even more importantly the equal relations between each member of society, including innovators, regulators, and publics. Innovators can be conceived as a broad group of actors, individuals, and organisations (e.g. scientists, entrepreneurs, firms, etc.) who are involved in the production of science, technology, and product/process innovations, pursuing novel ideas for commercialisation. In contrast, regulators are those individuals and regulatory bodies (e.g. policymakers, lawyers, industry experts, government agencies, etc.) which establish governance frameworks and constrains for de-risking and controlling technologies within specific sectors. Finally, publics are citizens and other users (e.g. interest groups, advocacy organisations, social movements, etc.) who resolve their everyday problems through technological innovation (Wield et al, 2017), and therefore improve their wellbeing.

Mitigating or eliminating relations of domination and oppression in the social process of generation and application of new knowledge should be the main objective of a non-ideal theory of justice in innovation and development. In fact, to achieve this objective, some level of equal share of new products and services (i.e. resources) is also required. Therefore, the latter is often a necessary condition for the former. Mitigation or elimination of relational inequality in innovation is very much influenced by mitigation or elimination of unjustified distributive inequality of resources.

To unpack the overall argument, this book is divided into six chapters. Although, some of these chapters have been already published in the form of articles at various research journals,[1] they have been updated and/or extensively revised for the purpose of this book. All chapters provide the logical steps towards the position defended in this book, namely that innovation and development can be just in non-ideal terms provided we focus on relations of equality among innovators, regulators, and publics. These are the main groups involved in processes of knowledge generation and exploitation. Chapter 1 is preoccupied with the modern idea of social justice. It provides a brief overview of key theories and argues that the idea of social justice ought to be predominantly relational and egalitarian, not just distributional. This chapter clarifies the interconnection between the two main aspects of justice in innovation (i.e. relations and resources), setting out the fundamental premises of my argument. In addition, it insists that public action is crucial for directing innovation and development towards just outcomes. Chapter 2 is focused on justice and innovation. It points out that relational social justice is a non-ideal standard and therefore pragmatist in nature. It is concerned with bottom-up processes of exploitation, oppression, and hierarchies which generate claims for egalitarian social justice in innovation. Applying the idea of relational justice in innovation allows for marginal inequality of material resources that functions as an incentive for novel products and services so long as it does not lead to inequality of social relations. Chapter 3 is focused on justice and development. It discusses the importance of development theory in understanding just social change driven by innovation. Concepts such as power, agency, scale, and history as well as schools of thought which consider development to be either a planned process or an unplanned process or a post-development process are crucial for establishing a comprehensive understanding of innovation and development. Chapter 4 examines the case of emerging technologies and asks the question of how these technologies can be evaluated from the point of view of relational justice in innovation. Chapter 5 puts forward the argument of directing innovation and development towards just outcomes. Such outcomes ought to be relational, taking everyone's interests and aspirations on board. Chapter 6 examines the role of the state in innovation and bottom-up alternatives. It defends a Poulantzian perspective of the state as a relationship of forces that is not static but evolving throughout history. From this perspective, it criticises contemporary notions of the so-called entrepreneurial state for lacking deep politico-theoretical foundations. The conclusion of this book summarises the overall argument of egalitarian justice in innovation and development as a relational approach to delivering fair outcomes.

Note

1 Chapters 2, 4, 5, and 6 draw on the following previous publications:
Papaioannou, T. (2020) 'Innovation, Value-Neutrality and the Question of Politics: Unmasking the Theoretical and Ideological Abuse of Evolutionary Theory' *Journal of Responsible Innovation*, Vol.7, No.2, pp.238–255. /www.mdpi.com/2071-1050/13/5/2655
Papaioannou, T. (2021) 'The Idea of Justice in Innovation: Applying Non-Ideal Political Theory to Address Questions of Sustainable Public Policy in Emerging Technologies' *Sustainability*, Vol.13, No.5, article no. 2655. www.mdpi.com/2071-1050/13/5/2655
Papaioannou, T. (2023) 'What Kind of Innovation State Matters for Social Justice? Learning from Poulantzas and Going Beyond' *Review of Evolutionary Political Economy*, Vol.4, pp.299–320. https://link.springer.com/article/10.1007/s43253-023-00099-6
Papaioannou, T. (2024) 'Directing Innovation Towards Just Outcomes: The Role of Principles and Politics' *Journal of Responsible Innovation*, Vol.11, No.1, pp.1–22. www.tandfonline.com/doi/epdf/10.1080/23299460.2024.2312623?needAccess=true

1 The Idea of Social Justice

A Brief Review of Theories

The modern idea of social justice is historically linked to successive scientific and technological revolutions which have introduced new products and services, paving the way to early industrialisation and development of Western societies. This is not to say, the modern idea of justice is universal. Non-Western societies have also developed (alternative) ideas of justice, competing with modern values of freedom and equality. For example, the idea of justice as 'ubuntu' that I will examine briefly later in this chapter demonstrates that there is a normative variety in the world. There are similarities and differences between ideas of justice which have been generated in different parts of the world. In the global South, justice appears to be akin to communitarianism whereas in the global North, the very same notion tends to defend individualism and negative freedom (freedom from something as opposed to freedom to something, i.e. positive). Brian Barry (2005), a well-known liberal theorist of social justice, argues that although until about a century and a half ago justice was generally understood as virtue of individuals, the early industrialisation of Britain and France in 1840s shifted the focus of justice on societies' institutions and social relations. This new focus points towards defining justice as an ideal that is about the institutional treatment of all kinds of inequalities, including distributional and relational inequalities. This treatment needs to be impartial, otherwise fairness might be compromised. The idea of 'justice as impartiality' defended by Barry and other liberal egalitarians in the Western, Rawlsian tradition of political thought requires '… taking everyone's situation and interests into account in determining what is to count as just outcome' (Wolff, 2006: 8). For example, to determine what is to count

DOI: 10.4324/9781003652083-2

as just outcome of distribution of innovative resources one needs to take into account the situation of everyone, including the situation of disabled people. Potential benefits for mobility and access will not be distributed fairly to everyone unless principles of justice guide public policy design.

Political theory has come up with various constructions to secure impartial answer to the question of 'how would you like it if you were in that situation?' (Wolff, 2006: 8). Constructivism, according to Barry, refers to '… two conditions: firstly, that what comes out of a certain situation is to be counted just, and secondly, that the construction is by the theorist and not by the people in the situation themselves' (Weale, 1998: 14). Both conditions are satisfied in the writings of liberal political theorists. Thus, Adam Smith's 'impartial spectator' who sympathises with someone's disadvantage (Smith, 1976) and John Rawls' 'veil of ignorance' that helps individuals to agree on impartial principles of distributive justice (Rawls, 1972) are the most well-known examples of constructivism in political theory. This constructivism means that, theoretically, no conception of the good is privileged or prioritised over others. This position has influenced public policy in the sense that it has enabled assessing the performance of specific innovation and development policy measures and schemes against ideal justice benchmarks. Yet, it has predominantly focused on distributive currencies of justice, i.e., various kinds of resources which ought to be shared in accordance with competing justifications. In doing so, it has overlooked relational injustices such as oppression, domination, exploitation, and hierarchies. Such injustices take place within society, creating multiple disadvantages for individuals and groups. The most important ones are exclusion and loss of self-respect and dignity.

This chapter argues that the non-ideal notion of social justice is first relational and then distributive. It is first relational because what matters for justice is to establish a society of equals in terms of respect, equity, recognition, and participation. It is then also distributive because relational equality as such often depends on fair share of material resources of society. These two analytically distinct but, at the same time, interrelated aspects of justice can enable normative evaluation of innovative and developmental activities within state borders and beyond them. Furthermore, they can provide the foundation of ethical analysis of innovation and development. As Ziegler (2015: 4) recognises, 'There is much to learn from this theory of justice for the ethical analysis of innovation, but only if we critically adapt the theory and the way it draws on economic theory to our time'.

In what follows, we first review key arguments and aspects of the theory and then attempt to adapt it in innovation and development. Contributions to ethical debate on innovation hitherto, have, for example, overwhelmingly focused on Rawlsian claims for distribution of resources. This chapter sides with Ziegler (Ziegler, 2015: 4) who argues that

> in contrast to the economic image drawn on by Rawls, the innovation process is bigger, differently structured, and relevant for justice beyond focus on monetary gains to be redistributed. Once this is realised, innovation for justice points to more rather than less equality, as well as a two-fold innovation focus – on improvement for the least advantaged today as well as the long-term stability of society.

1.1 Distributive Justice

Let me start with the set of basic ideas of distributive justice. These are ideas about how material resources such as income and wealth and technologies ought to be distributed to different members of society in a just way. In what follows, I provide overview of three ideas: justice as free and equal distribution; justice as free and unequal distribution; and justice as utility.

Justice as Free and Equal Distribution

This idea of justice is centred at the liberal notion of fairness that applies to free and equal individuals as well as to their institutions. Liberty is defined as the absence of coercion in making choices about different things in life and conception of the good. Equality is defined as fair equality of opportunity for everyone, independently of race, gender, and class.

Proponents of the liberal egalitarian idea of justice such as John Rawls derive their theories from the contractarian traditions of Locke and Kant. Thus, they formally advance two fundamental principles from a hypothetical 'original position' of choice (Rawls, 1972). The original position is Rawls' innovative solution to the problem of fair and impartial development of egalitarian principles of justice. As such, this contractarian theoretical device competes with other approaches, e.g., utilitarianism, providing the logical foundations for the principles of distributive justice. According to Rawls, everyone in the hypothetical original position could chose principles of justice behind a 'veil of ignorance' by asking the following question: what provisions for the poor or the disadvantaged (including the technologically poor or disadvantaged) would I chose in my society if I did not know whether or not I was poor or disadvantaged? Rawls argues that without knowing one's situation in life, or where one would end up after choosing principles of justice from an impartial position, we could all agree on a fair idea of justice that can be guided by the following principles: first, everyone has the same political rights and basic liberties; second, the distribution of economic and social inequalities should benefit everyone and especially the least advantaged members of society (Rawls, 1999). Rawls calls his first principle of justice as *Equal Liberty* in order to emphasise his equalitarian liberal approach to justice. According to Chandler (2023: 8) 'This first principle – the 'basic liberties principle' – is what makes Rawls's theory distinctively liberal, and it provides the basis for designing a democratic institution and political system'. He then terms his second principle as *Difference Principle* to emphasise that not everyone in society is the same and that inequalities which are a matter of choice (i.e. those to the greatest benefit of the least well-off) are morally and politically acceptable in society. This second principle defines Rawls's egalitarian approach to resources. It demands that basic institutions of society and economy should be organised in such way that the living conditions of the least well off are improved. According to Chandler (Chandler, 2023: 39; italics added) 'For Rawls, the difference principle was ultimately grounded in a spirit of reciprocity, or even *fraternity* that we should only want some people to have more than others if this also benefits those who have less'. The main point of Rawls's principles is to provide a normative framework within which individual preferences and potential conflicts of individual values and interests can be regulated.

The focus of Rawls' distributive principles of justice is on the overall structure of society, the creation of social and political institutions which can promote one liberal scheme of fair co-operation (Chandler, 2023: 54). In this co-operative scheme the outcome of a distributive arrangement of what Rawls calls 'primary goods', i.e., rights, liberties, income, and wealth, is considered to be fair or just when it satisfies the two fundamental principles which people mutually agreed in the original position, i.e., *Equal Liberty* and *Difference Principle*. If a distributive arrangement fails to satisfy these two principles, then government should step in to redistribute 'primary goods' in a way that can make the worst off as well off as possible (Rawls, 1999). Clearly, Rawls believes that inequalities require justification by the potential benefits they can bring to the least advantaged members of society (Callinicos, 2000). In addition, he thinks that justified inequalities function as incentives for people to do jobs in demand, encouraging innovation and growth. For example, high wages in specific technological sectors, e.g., biotech, artificial intelligence (AI), etc., can attract high-skilled people and therefore promote the generation of products and services.

Rawls' idea of justice is not, of course, uncontested. Since the first publication of his *A Theory of Justice* (1972), several critiques have consistently focused on the inadequacy of his arguments, advancing alternative theories of equalitarian justice (Scanlon, 1982; Barry, 1995). For example, it's rather impossible to achieve consensus on principles of justice in real historical terms. People have different considerations of fairness given their backgrounds and their circumstances from which Rawls' original position abstracts for the sake of argument. Achieving an 'overlapping consensus' between people who disagree over fairness assumes several conditions, including a high level of reasoning and understanding of the interests of free and equal people. These assumptions are risky given the complexity of society as a whole. On top of this problem, there seems to be no proper justification of the choice of primary goods as the basis of interpersonal comparisons. Finally, Rawls focuses on the basic structure of society, i.e., institutions of liberal constitutional democracies and in doing so he overlooks claims of injustice at the level of individuals or assumes that fixing institutions will automatically address claims of social justice.

For Rawls, distributive justice is predominantly a task for the state alone and not for individuals. The state, by accepting inequality that improves the situation of the worst off, maintains incentives for the better off. This incentive consideration, according to Cohen (2008: 15)

> produces an argument for inequality that presupposes a model of society as non-community, in which relations among human beings are construed as strategic, with people taking one another into account as so many opportunities for and, obstacles to, gain,

rather than as fellow citizens by whom they can be asked to justify the way they live.

This instrumental regard of individuals for others is in contradistinction with relational egalitarianism and communitarian philosophies of the global South such as Ubuntu. These philosophies deny the claim that economic inequalities within and between countries actually benefit the worst off. In fact, they argue that progressively exacerbate the gap between rich and poor in the world.

Yet, Rawls' theory is still regarded as the greatest work of twentieth century political philosophy. The most recent reconstruction of his liberal egalitarian justice by Chandler (2023) suggests that it is still very influential among many theorists and practitioners. Chandler's aim is '… to use Rawls's theory to construct 'a realistic utopia': to describe a set of institutions that are the best we can hope for, given what we know about human nature and the constraints of natural world' (Chandler, 2023: 14). However, as I will show in this book, applying an ideal theory of justice in innovation and development is rather a problematic task. Instead, the focus should be on relational aspects of justice which are by definition non-ideal and require empirical investigation.

Justice as Free and Unequal Distribution

This is the so-called right-wing libertarian idea of justice; it is founded upon the notion of inviolable or absolute individual rights. According to Robert Nozick (1974: ix), one of Rawls's contemporaries, 'Individuals have rights, and there are things no person or group may do to them (without violating their rights)'. Libertarians often invoke Kant's third version of the Categorical Imperative (i.e. *Act in such a way that you always treat humanity, whether in your own person or in the person of any other, never simply as a means, but always at the same time as an end*) to insist that justice only applies to free individuals. As such, free individuals have absolute rights over themselves, their talents and capacities and their property. This implies they can do whatever they like with themselves, their talents and capacities, and their property as long as they respect the right of others to do the same.

For Nozick, individual rights are 'side constraints' that protect individuals from state policies which promote equal distribution of resources. According to his theory, equal distribution of resources through the basic structure of society violates individual rights and especially the right to self-ownership, i.e., '… every person is morally entitled to full private property in his person and powers. This means that each person has an extensive set of moral rights … over the use and fruits of his body and capacities …' (Cohen and Graham, 1990: 25). To put it another way, society is not justified to claim any form of property over persons. Even though persons are born and realise themselves in society, they don't owe anything to it as far as Nozick is concerned.

On the grounds of self-ownership and moral inviolability of persons, libertarians such as Nozick (1974: 151) argue that if the world was just, the following principles would guide justice in holdings: first everyone who acquires a holding such as income and wealth that came about by permissible action (e.g. hard work) s/he is entitled to that holding; second, everyone who acquires a holding is free to transfer it in exchange for something else or as a gift and this is just transfer; third, no one is entitled to a holding except by repeated applications of the first and second principles. Entitlements are historical in the sense that an existing holding will be just if it arises from an act of initial acquisition or repeated acts of just transfer. Nozick calls his first principle as *Acquisition Principle* to emphasise initial acquisition of unowned resources. He terms his second principle as *Transfer Principle* to emphasise exchange of justly owned resources such income and wealth through the free market. Finally, Nozick calls his third principle of justice as *Historical Principle* to stress that whenever there is unjust taking of a just holding, the state is justified to intervene to rectify the injustice. These three principles justify a minimal state that is tasked with protection of absolute individual rights. A minimal state can only have narrow functions such as protection against force, theft and enforcement contracts. Anything more than that would violate individual rights. Therefore, the state ought to be a 'night-watchman' institution that could tax citizens for paying police, army and public servants to protect property rights and contracts in the market.

More recently, critiques of the libertarian tradition of political thought such as Chandler (2023: 78) argue that 'Nozick's views are pretty extreme: they put him on the far-right branch of the liberal family tree and it's hard to find anyone in politics today who takes such a hard line about absolute priority of property rights'. Indeed, even within the free and unequal distribution camp, most theorists accept the basic role of the state as provider of some basic public goods and social welfare. For example, Hayek (1960) does not deny such provisions are important for enabling individuals to re-enter the market and learn from the disappointment of their initial expectations. In this sense, he attributes the state a specific role for developing a basic safety net for individual persons who risk their participation in the market. For Nozick, however, the responsibility for such safety net lies with responsible individuals. Individual responsibility had clearly escaped attention of the Rawlsian tradition.

Nozick's theory of justice has received strong criticism from egalitarian liberals in the Rawlsian tradition. The main focus of this criticism over the decades has been on the principle of 'self-ownership' that overlooks the role of society in shaping individual talents and capacities for acquiring resources. Individuals do not necessarily deserve their talents and capacities in absolute terms simply because society is partly responsible for their (under) development. Individuals are embedded in society and in turn, society is embedded in individuals. Therefore, individuals cannot be absolute beneficiaries of the fruits of their talents and capacities. Instead, they ought to allow redistribution of resources to compensate for those who were not lucky enough to be born with talents or with resources to develop capacities.

Justice as Utility

Both liberal egalitarian and libertarian ideas of justice can be seen as rights-based responses to utilitarianism. The latter is a genuine third theory to contrast with justice as equal distribution and justice as unequal distribution. Utilitarianism claims that people ought to act in such a way that they maximise general happiness of society or welfare or social good. Utilitarianism is a consequentialist tradition of political morality. This means that it is interested in whether the consequences of human action, including policy and practice of innovation, maximise or minimise happiness (Kymlicka, 1990). In this respect, utilitarianism is a 'bottom-up' theory of justice. It starts off with the desired consequences of human action and moves on to appropriate rules and/or public policies whereas justice as free and unequal distribution is a 'top-down' theory, justifying rules and policies independently of consequences of human action. To put it another way, utilitarianism is indeed a theory of the 'good' (that can be evaluated on the grounds of the consequences of rules and policies) whereas justice as unequal distribution is a theory of 'the right' (that can be evaluated on the grounds of the plausibility of values and policies, regardless the consequences). For utilitarians, the good is about happiness or utility (or want satisfaction).

The founding fathers of utilitarianism, Bentham (1970) and Mill (1937), conceive happiness as a sum of pleasures. Pleasure is morally good and pain is morally bad (Raphael, 2001). As Dworkin (1977: 160) points out, utilitarianism is a goal-based theory of justice concerned with the welfare or well-being of each individual. Therefore, this theory is competing with right-based theories of justice, including Rawls' egalitarian liberalism and Nozick's libertarianism. For utilitarians, individual rights are just legal obligations which contribute to maximisation of the aggregate utility (Lyons, 1984). Bentham (1970: 11–12) defines utility as the '… principle which approves or disapproves of every action whatsoever, according to the tendency which it appears to have augment or diminish the happiness of the party whose interest is in question …'.

Some contemporary defenders of liberalism argue that, in fact, the doctrine of right derives from the liberal conception of the good. Others, e.g., Barry (1995) insist that the liberal doctrine of right is a free-standing doctrine and therefore independent of conflicting conceptions of the good. Neutrality on the good feeds to a fundamental conception of justice as impartiality. In any case, the good for contemporary utilitarians translates into welfare maximization, i.e., a persons' preferences for some innovations, services, etc., over others. Individuals are rational actors who try to satisfy their preferences in the market, maximising the aggregate utility of society.

Utilitarianism is popular with policymakers because it justifies focus on growth through entrepreneurship and innovation. Thus, as Ziegler (2020: 69) points out '… the utilitarian philosophy offers no grounds to rule out the sacrifice of some, including the violation of liberty of some, as long as this increases the overall good'. Quite often both innovation and development policy decisions are defended on the grounds of beneficial consequences for most of the population, overlooking risks for the minority of local communities and/or ignoring their human rights. Utilitarianism does not require equal distribution of rewards and risks of innovation. If unequal distribution of new technologies satisfies the rich to the extent that the dissatisfaction of the poor is outweighed, then the overall sum is positive and so utilitarians have no reason to insist on more equal distribution. In fact, utilitarians support the increase of general welfare of society through technological innovation at the expense of individual members of that society. For example, utilitarians are comfortable with the increase of general welfare of society through emerging technology applications at the expense of individual members who lose their jobs due to automation and machine learning. Yet, the whole idea of innovation systems that emphasises institutional linkages for the sake of innovation is based on utilitarianism. The expectation is that such linkages will maximise learning through interaction and thereby increase innovation, impacting positively on aggregate utility.

1.2 Relational Justice

Let me now turn to the set of ideas I can call relational justice. These are ideas about how relations between people ought to be arranged in a just way so that no one is excluded, oppressed, exploited, or discriminated against others. Relational justice is based on the premise that the equal (or unequal) distribution of resources alone (e.g. provision of novel technological goods, infrastructure and services) will not address phenomena of oppression, exploitation or discrimination. As Fourie et al (2015: 7) observe

> Social egalitarians often distance themselves from an emphasis on distribution as being primary concern of egalitarianism. While social equality is likely to have significant implications for distribution, many egalitarians insist that social equality cannot be captured foremost according to a description of the distribution of goods or some other currency.

Roughly speaking, ideas of relational justice encompass: justice as equal respect; justice as recognition and participation; justice as capability; and justice as ubuntu.

Justice as Equal Respect

Relational egalitarianism is a contemporary approach to justice that derives directly from 'critical oppositional activity' (Young, 2001: 671) against power structures which promote unequal respect, oppression, and domination in society. This marks a substantial analytical difference with Rawls' egalitarian liberalism that derives justice from an imagined original position. In justice as equal respect, the focus is on the activist who fights injustice not only at the level individual wrongs and repressive public policies, but also at the level of social structures which threaten large groups of persons with domination and/or oppression. For Iris Marion Young (2011), this is a phenomenon of structural injustice that often occurs as an unintended consequence of many individuals and social institutions acting to achieve their particular objectives and serve their interests within a framework of accepted values and norms. To address structural injustice as well as repressive public policies, activism is essential. According to Iris Marion Young (Young, 2011: 673):

> Besides being motivated by passion for justice, the activist is often also propelled by anger or frustration at what he judges is the intransigence of people in power in existing institutions, who behave with arrogance and indifference toward the injustices the activist finds they perpetuate or flatly deny them and rationalise their decisions and institutions they serve as beneficial.

For Young (1990) these injustices do not concern the narrow maldistribution of resources such as income and wealth but the wide relational context within which such maldistribution exists. Unjust distributive arrangements of benefits and burdens are due to underlying social, political, cultural symbolic, and institutional conditions. These conditions simply demonstrate lack of respect and recognition of culturally and racially diverse people who end up devaluated and insulted. In Young's view, the people who are the most affected by structural injustice share responsibility to challenge and eventually eliminate such oppressive conditions. Change is a matter of collective action and not individual heroism.

From a relational perspective of justice, issues of (re) distribution are crucial but incomplete unless issues of social relations are addressed. Elizabeth Anderson (1999, 2010) takes Young's argument forward by providing a relational theory of justice. Her criticism is directed against recent liberal egalitarian approaches to social justice which, as she says, have lost sight of the distinctively political aims of egalitarianism. The first aim of egalitarian justice is to end socially imposed oppression. The second aim is to create a community in which people stand in relations of equality to others. According to Anderson, a relational theory of justice is a non-ideal theory that investigates claims of relational injustice first and then considers appropriate policies to rectify. The latter is a process of trial and error; it involves different policy measures and schemes which are tried on the ground to establish whether they work. In other words, Anderson as well as other contemporary theorists (e.g. Mantouvalou and Wolff, 2024) seem to believe that activism is not the only path to just social change. Government policies and the rule of law are so important forces of change.

Justice as Recognition and Participation

Justice as recognition is closely associated with relational egalitarianism. It has been introduced by Nancy Fraser and Alex Honneth (2003) who consider claims for legal or cultural recognition and claims for political representation to be crucial for achieving equality of social relations. For Fraser and Honneth, misrecognition and lack of participation are tied to institutional inequity. Thus, their focus is on the structured nature of disrespected identities and communities.

In this sense, the recognition and participation approach are placed alongside distributive theories of justice. According to Fraser (2003: 7–8) 'The discourse of social justice, once centred on distribution is now increasingly divided between claims for redistribution on the one hand and claims for recognition on the other'. Both redistribution and recognition are required in social arrangements for achieving just outcomes. In Fraser's view, it is philosophically defensible to integrate redistribution and recognition in one normative paradigm that aims to equalise relations between people, their societies and environments.

The remedy for social injustice clearly includes changes in the basic economic structures. But it also includes recognising cultural diversity and transforming patterns of representation in ways that everyone's identity and interests are taken on board. For Fraser, this distinction between redistributive remedies and recognition remedies is not substantive but analytical. In fact, redistributive remedies presuppose recognition remedies (Fraser, 2008).

Justice as Capability

The capability approach is also a response to the distributive ideas of liberal egalitarianism, libertarianism, and utilitarianism. These ideas have been predominantly about institutions which influence our lives through distribution of resources. Liberal egalitarians such as Rawls, libertarians such as Nozick and utilitarians such as Bentham are concerned about justice of institutions as opposed to justice of individuals (e.g. individual lives, actions, etc.). That's exactly where Sen's critique is being directed. Even if social institutions (what Rawls called 'basic structure') are just, individuals might still face injustices because they are not necessarily capable of using the equal resources the institutions provide for being and doing what they want. Sen criticises Rawls for taking political philosophy to the wrong direction (Chandler, 2023). As Chandler (2023: 97) observes,

> Sen's starting point is that political philosophy should offer us practical guidance about how we can address injustices in our own societies. In particular, a theory of justice should help us to compare and ultimately decide between the different policy choices that we actually faced with here and now.

In the *Tanner Lectures on Human Values*, Sen (1980) asserts that what matters in the discussion of social justice is not the question of 'why equality' but the question of 'equality of what?' Answering this latter question provides the so called 'currency' of Senian justice which is capability (Sen, 1999). The capability approach that has been also endorsed by Nussbaum (2006, 2000) shifts focus from the basic structure of society to the basic freedoms of people. In Sen's and Nussbaum's views, resources, including income, wealth, and the environment, are merely the means to freedom for people to choose different kinds of life. This is what the notion of capability refers to: each individual's actual freedom to achieve the functioning he/she values (leading an autonomous and meaningful life). Capabilities are about each individual's opportunities to do and be what they choose in society. Therefore, the focus is on individual agency and well-being.

Sen and Nussbaum arrive at the idea of capability partly through their critical assessment of Rawlsian primary goods. Their dissatisfaction with Rawlsian primary goods is founded upon the realisation that some individuals are differently capable of converting them into well-being or welfare because of variations in a range of factors, including biology and social conditions. For example, disabled, women, and other disadvantaged people cannot achieve the same level of well-being as advantaged people with the same amount of primary goods, including material goods. The point for Sen and Nussbaum is to examine what we are able to do with those goods. To put it another way, material goods as such do not matter; what matters is what individuals are able to do with them. For Sen the ultimate concern is capabilities which are the result of relations between persons and goods like wealth. By equalising capabilities, Sen is enabling freedom of choice. Individuals can actively engage with the world in accordance with their aspirations to be and do what they want.

Several theorists argue that the idea of justice as capability can accommodate both distributive and relational concerns. They also stress that this idea of justice can be extended to groups and/or communities.

Justice as Ubuntu

The set of predominantly Western ideas of relational justice that I have briefly discussed so far, is in line with other traditions of non-Western cultures. One of them is the ubuntu philosophy in Africa. The contribution of this philosophy to debates of relational justice and development is important. Ubuntu is based on the premise that one's essence is being rooted in one's relationships and interconnectedness with others. Therefore, moral roles, commitments, and obligations of social justice emanate from these relationships and are guided by principles of reciprocity and the pursue of common good. The African notion of common good is different from the Western European notion of common good. While the latter is about '... the aggregate of particular goods of individual persons, which like individual rights, ought to be respected' (Gyekye, 1997: 13), the former is about the good that is common to all human beings. This understanding of common good is linked to the concept of common humanity and cannot be possibly derived from individual conceptions of the good (Gyekye, 1997: 13).

To put it another way, ubuntu is a communitarian approach to social justice. It is underpinned by values of co-operation and collaboration. In this sense, it rejects individualism for the sake of communal relationships. It is only within the community that human worth can be recognised. As Munyaradzi and Mubaya (2016: 92) put it '... it is the group and not the individuals that motivate daily endeavours, design and behaviour'. This focus on groups (as opposed the focus on individuals) can be considered counter-hegemonic in the sense of coming from the bottom-up to challenge hegemonic narratives of liberalism which are centred in individualism.

Ubuntu as a term derives from Nguni and Banta languages in Sub-Saharan Africa. It signifies 'being human' and this can only happen in a community of humans. This does not imply that individual freedom is subordinated but that individuals are free to pursue their own conceptions of the good through pursuing the common good. From this it follows that human nature is special and inviolable due to its capacity for harmonious relationships. At the same time, no individual's rights are greater than another, thus, every individual in a community including both children and adults is important and should be heard and respected'.

Although the idea of justice as ubuntu is contributing a relational perspective of fairness from the global South, it has been overlooked in contemporary philosophical debates about just innovation and development, e.g., ethical obligations of emerging technologies. This is, of course, not surprising given the dominance of western liberal theories of justice in such debates about ethics and new technologies. For instance, Roche et al (2023) provide clear evidence for the prevalence of global North and liberal ethical concerns across AI literatures. This will become apparent later in the book. In what follows, I will assume ubuntu as part of a wider relational approach to justice in innovation. Along with relational justice theorists such as Anderson, Fraser, and Sen, proponents of justice as ubuntu can play crucial role in helping us understand the moral obligations of innovators of emerging technologies.

1.3 Justice and Public Action

Often ideas of social justice appear to focus on institutional solutions to issues of poverty and inequality. For example, they rely on state and non-state organisations, including UN agencies, for distribution of resources. This is very much in abstraction from power relations and global structures which generate poverty and inequality in the first place. Yet such unequal relations and structures are confronted by public actions and social movements which aim to overcome the subordination of the poor worldwide. Public actions and social movements are '... considerably wider than the actions of the state' (Mackintosh, 1992: 4) and imply purposive collective actions for collective public ends (Papaioannou, 2014). Such ends are framed as just or legitimate ends. Therefore, public actions and social movements put forward claims of relational justice through organised mechanisms but also through ad hoc and informal practices (Grugel et al, 2017).

Take for example the set of public actions which have come to be defined as grassroots or below the radar innovation (BRI) for low-income community development (Smith et al, 2017). This includes low-and-middle-income groups which draw on indigenous knowledge and networks of other activists in order to introduce low-tech innovations that solve practical problems in local communities and meet basic needs. Such innovations might represent incremental changes in existing technological products. However, as has been argued elsewhere (Kaplinsky et al, 2009: 191):

> a key feature of BRI is the collective significance of these various developments underlying innovation as a process. The likelihood, therefore, is for the development of new products in regions such China and India aimed at these low-income markets. The product-process linkage inherent in many sectors ... leads to a clustering of production technologies which are similarly reflective of operating conditions in these low-income markets.

Advanced globalisation in the past decade has helped some of these products to enter low-income markets such as those of Sub-Saharan Africa and Latin America. In this sense, grassroots or BRI scaled up in certain developmental contexts.

Apart from the large value of grassroots or BRI for low-income local communities, such low-tech innovations are potentially disruptive of global innovation hierarchies. This is not so much because of the introduction of new technologies but because of the new types of consumers which induce grassroots or BRI. As has been stressed elsewhere (Kaplinsky et al, 2009: 192) the existing innovation leaders:

> are unable to either recognise or exploit these new opportunities. Their trajectories and market antennae inhibit them from fully recognising these new opportunities which are 'below the radar'. Their cost structure – with regard to not just their core component technologies, but also the structure of their value chains – makes it difficult to address these markets, even if they are recognised.

The OECD (2012) but also Smith et al (2017) have listed a number of cases of grassroots or BRI. I have done the same in previous work

(Papaioannou, 2018), specifically analysing the cases of the Indian *Honeybee Network* (HBN) and the Brazilian *Social Technologies Network* (RTS). The former has identified and documented hundreds of grassroots innovations while the latter has introduced low-cost solutions to poor communities improving peoples' livelihoods.

Whether one looks at the actions of HBN in India or the innovations of RTS in Brazil, the thing that becomes clear is this: initiatives from 'below' have introduced low-tech innovations which embody relational principles of justice as alternatives to high-tech innovations from the top-down which fail to meet the requirements of justice in innovation. Indeed, empirical research diagnoses that innovations from 'above' ranging from automobiles and digital technologies to genomics and biotechnologies often exclude the very poor, thereby increasing inequalities, spreading starvation, violence and despair around the world (Papaioannou, 2018). The main reason for this exclusion is the process of innovation from 'above' that is often hierarchical, undemocratic and it is driven by short-term profit-making incentives which side-line principles of equity, recognition, and participation. This process of 'innovation from above' often delivers growth but leaves disadvantaged individuals and communities behind. These individuals and their communities are restricted in terms of access by prohibited prices and intellectual property regulations. In addition, they are often excluded by the complexity of high technologies. Schumacher (1973, 1979) recognised that such technologies might be inappropriate for the poor. For this reason, he argued for the importance of 'intermediate technologies' which meet peoples' basic needs. In this sense, innovation from above fails to promote sustainability of the whole of economy and society. It leads to products and processes which are not necessarily useful or affordable to people who live in low-income countries. The injustice can be addressed by grassroots innovation movements.

1.4 Concluding Remarks

This first chapter of the book at hand has argued that the idea of social justice as such is both relational and distributive. Establishing a society in which people relate equally to each other, presupposes a certain threshold of equal distribution of resources. The threshold can be only determined by the level of equality of relations in such society. The application of justice in innovation very much depends on public action. Through grassroots innovation movements and networks, relational principles emerge as a normative framework within which a plurality of innovative products and processes provide solutions to low-income societies. Some of these products even manage to scale up in certain developmental contexts. The so-called grassroots or BRI constitute counter-hegemonic alternatives to top-down and exclusive innovations of big multinational companies. Their aim is not only to provide technical solutions to logical problems but also put forward a political vision of relational egalitarian technological change.

2 Justice and Innovation

The liberal egalitarian and libertarian and utilitarian ideas of social justice which I briefly examined in the previous chapter have been constructivist in nature. This implies political theorists' attempt to construct and justify ideal principles of justice and then to use them as a normative benchmarking framework within which to evaluate individual and social action and institutions. Especially political theories of distributive justice have used non-historically founded theoretical devices such as Rawls' original position to justify principles of fairness and identify the gap between an ideal just world and a non-ideal unjust reality. Closing this gap through public policy and/or activism is rather impossible. Measures for distribution and redistribution of material resources depend on the non-ideal reality of capitalist economic production as well as on the limited knowledge of individual circumstances. Ideal theories of justice fail to account for scientific facts in economy and society. Therefore, they are unable to guide human action in pragmatic moral terms when it comes to real-world circumstances.

Constructivism in political theory has recently been criticised for its ideal nature, prompting the formation of a countermovement of non-ideal theory of social justice. Among others, authors such as Sen (2009) and Andersen (1999, 2010) claim that normative theorising about justice cannot be based on constructions or philosophical devices which are fact insensitive to empirical reality. For example, Sen considers such constructions and devices to be

> 'transcendental' in the sense that they develop a detailed picture of a perfectly just society, rather than being 'comparative' in which

DOI: 10.4324/9781003652083-3

> case they would help us compare and choose between different policies and institutions. While imagining a perfectly just society might be an interesting philosophical exercise ... it is largely irrelevant in practice.
>
> (Chandler, 2023: 97)

Instead of ideal theorising, justice can be based on empirically true assumptions which succeed to pass a feasibility test, i.e., a test conducted to provide evidence of whether a theory is feasible in real world. The aim of such non-ideal theorising should be to mitigate current injustices instead of moving us from the current unjust state of the world to a perfectly just one (Volacu, 2018). Non-ideal theorists consider a perfectly just world to be empirically impossible. Therefore, they focus their efforts on mitigating injustices through targeted interventions. The latter range from re-distribution of resources and social policy to enabling the disadvantaged to have recognition and participation in specific social and political processes.

This chapter is focused on the ideal versus the non-ideal approach to social justice in innovation. It defends a non-ideal social justice as a more realist or pragmatic approach to delivering just outcomes of innovation. In doing so, it accepts that there is no such thing as a 'perfect' theory of justice in innovation; instead, there are innovation injustices in the actual world. Hence this chapter discusses normative principles and values generated from the bottom-up through every day public action and campaigning to respond to relational injustices. The next section will defend the notion of non-ideal justice on relational grounds arguing that there is a need for systematic empirical investigations of claims of domination and oppression in society. Section 2 will apply non-ideal relational justice in innovation arguing that technical and technological change ought to be governed by non-ideal principles emerging through public action especially in developmental contexts. These principles are: equity, recognition, and participation. Section 2.3 will analyse the fundamental implications of this normative discussion for innovation policy.

2.1 Defending Non-Ideal Justice

In an article that contrasts ideal with non-ideal theory, Valentini (2012) distinguishes between three meanings given to adjectives 'ideal' and 'non-ideal'. First, ideal theory is taken to mean 'full compliance' with demands of justice whereas non-ideal theory is taken to mean 'partial compliance'. Second, ideal theory is taken to mean 'utopian theory' whereas non-ideal theory is taken to mean 'realistic theory'. Finally, ideal theory is taken to mean 'end-state theory' whereas non-ideal theory is taken to mean 'transitional theory'. It might be argued that all three meanings are relevant for understanding different aspects of the normative debate, including compliance, feasibility, and dynamism. The understanding of justice as a timeless/fact free principle that faces no constraints of reality is rather a-historical and perhaps unable to guide public policy. Ideal justice is constructed through abstract theorising without 'contamination' of empirical/historical facts. Its theoretical ambition is to provide a kind of pure normative guidance to politics and society. This implies holding politics and society to account for not complying with such normative index of ideal principles. The implication is highly problematic. In fact, non-ideal politics and society can only be held to account for not complying with non-ideal principles. This is why, in contrast, non-ideal justice is formulated through concrete empirical/historical investigation of claims of relational inequality. Its ambition is to facilitate the development of a society of equals. This implies tailoring public policies towards addressing objectionable relational inequalities such as domination, hierarchy, exploitation, and paternalism which have been identified on the ground and enabling excluded or marginalised people to equalise their relations with others.

Although non-ideal theory at first glance appears to be somewhat less ambitious than ideal theory, it takes on board issues of partial compliance with principles of justice and unfavourable circumstances. Anderson (2010) explains this in terms of the imperfections of human beings. According to her 'A system of principles that would produce a just world if they regulated the conduct of perfectly rational and just persons will not do so when we ask human beings, with all our limitations and flaws, to follow them' (Anderson, 2010: 3–4). It is such motivational and cognitive deficiencies in human beings which point towards the importance of empirical investigation and diagnosis of the underlying causes of injustices and then the development of a non-ideal theory that could provide concrete solutions to problems. As Anderson (Anderson, 2010: 6) puts it:

> Non-ideal theory begins with a diagnosis of the problems and complains of our society and investigates how to overcome these

> problems. Non-ideal theory does not dispense with ideals but conceives of their function differently from ideal theory. In ideal theory, ideals function as standards of assessment for any society … In non-ideal theory, ideals embody imagined solutions to identified problems in society.

Such solutions might be implemented or tried on the ground so that they can mitigate or even eliminate injustices. In this sense, non-ideal theory turns to be more effective in terms of guiding agency in empirically contingent circumstances. It can function as a set of hypotheses to be tested in the real world. According to Anderson (2010):

> We test our ideals by putting them into practice and seeing whether they solve the problems for which they were devised, settle people's reasonable complaints, and offer a way of life that people find superior to what they had before. If they pass the test, this does not validate them outside history. Circumstances change, and new problems and complaints arise, requiring the construction of new ideals. If our ideals fail the test, we need to revise or replace them.

This constant empirical testing of imagined solutions to problems of social justice constitutes the main methodology of non-ideal theory. Instead of using abstract ideals as standards of social and political assessment, this theory uses ideals as social and political tests of reality. Although it's an open question whether such reality is the same for everyone, there are common perceptions of the social and political world in several respects. For example, there are common perceptions of social and political oppression within certain marginalised groups. These are common perceptions of exploitation within certain social classes, e.g., working classes.

Certainly, a non-ideal theory of justice is not uncontested. One criticism has been that it is difficult to separate such theory from ideal approaches to justice simply because contemporary political theorists tend to display features of both (Ypi, 2012). Another criticism has been that neither ideal theory nor non-ideal theory alone is sufficient for meeting the overall goal of designing just institutions (Volacu, 2018). Both criticisms lead to the argument that ideal and non-ideal theories need to be combined. For Ypi (2012) the alternative of ideal/non-ideal combination is about the pursuing of normative theory in an activist mode that she calls 'dialectical'. This theory emphasises the development of relationship between principles and agency. According to Ypi (2012: 41):

> The circumstances of particular conflicts and the analysis of existing social practices lead theorists and other agents occupying relevant social roles to reflect on them and to articulate specific interpretations of the concerns and commitments they express. After various stages of revision and having obtained some basic level of plausibility, these interpretations are combined with certain first-order value and give rise to fundamentally appropriate theories, theories that are in turn invoked to guide political action.

Implicitly, Ypi seems to accept the ideal theory's claim that first-order values cannot directly derive from public action. Thus, she implies that such values remain privileged products of some kind of 'pure' moral thinking that can then be combined with articulated interpretations of empirical concerns about social and political issues (Papaioannou, 2018). Similarly, for Volacu (2018) we need ideal theory in order to assess what a perfectly just state of the world looks like but at the same time we also need a bridge for transition to non-ideal theory to assess how we can move from our unjust world to a comparatively just one. Volacu does not seem to explain why ideal assessments of the world are necessary given that they are both fact-insensitive and infeasible. It may be the case that ideal assessments of the world are inspirational or put forward a vision that can motivate action towards improvement. However, the question remains: why would institutional designers waste time to begin their assessment from ideal level and then transit to non-ideal level? Wouldn't be better for them to begin from empirical investigation and diagnosis of injustices on the ground and then transit to the level of agency? It might be argued that the main shortcoming of Volacu's argument is lack of agency in the continuum between ideal and non-ideal theory.

More recent defenders of ideal theory such as Chandler (2023) argue that we need ideal theory to use as a target or indeed as a normative benchmark for evaluating existing institutions. In addition, we need ideal theory to provide us with a set of values with which to choose among relevant policies of redistribution. However, it is clear that neither ideal targets/benchmarks (developed without the participation of relevant stakeholders) nor ideal values (developed in transcendental way) can provide a pragmatic moral framework within which to assess and address claims of injustice in society. Such claims are predominantly about unequal social relations and not only about unequal resources.

Agency is, of course, the main focus of non-ideal theories of relational justice, ranging from Young to ubuntu theorists. For instance, Sen (2009: x) stresses that the idea of justice '… is ultimately connected with the way peoples' lives go …' and whether they can become capable to be and do what they chose. However, his notion of 'agency freedom' mainly includes goals of individual well-being and not goals of political agency that are focused on changing social relations and institutions in accordance with demands of justice. Although Sen (2009) responds to his critiques rejecting that he is methodologically individualist, he also admits that his primary concern is agency of persons and not of groups. This has implications for public action that is focused on addressing relational and institutional injustices. Oppressive and paternalistic social `relations and institutions through which people exercise power, dominate, exploit, and marginalise others can mainly be changed through collective agency, including campaigns and actions of social movements (Papaioannou, 2018). A non-ideal theory of justice should therefore subscribe to pragmatism by endorsing public action and campaigning as important means of change.

Public action emerges when empirical identification and causal explanation of injustice raises the question of '… what can and ought to be done about it, and who should be charged with correcting it' (Anderson, 2010: 22). This requires both evaluation and attribution of political responsibility for change (Anderson, 2010). In terms of evaluation, it might be argued that judgements about social injustices can be based on normative reflections which are both historically and socially contextualised. This is what Young (1990: 5) regards as 'critical theory'. In her view, 'Critical theory presumes that normative ideals used to criticise society are rooted in experience of and reflection on that very society, and that norms can come from nowhere else'. Clearly, when norms are not founded upon public action, they are incapable of guiding towards a morally accepted direction. Instead, they carry empty ideals which contain no experience or critical reflection on social injustices.

Young's critical theory and Anderson's non-ideal theory converge in several points but one of them is key: their understanding of normative principles of justice as bottom-up developments of public action. Young (2001: 672–673) describes the typical public activist as follows:

> The activist is committed to social justice and normative value and the idea that politically responsible persons ought to take positive action to promote these. He also believes that the normal workings of the social, economic and political institutions in which he dwells enact or reproduce deep wrongs – some laws or policies have unjust effects or social and economic structures cause injustice, or non-human animals and things are wrongly endangered and so on. The activist opposes particular actions and policies of public or private institutions as well as systems of policies or actions and wants them changed.

By contesting relations of power, domination and oppression, public activists generate egalitarian principles of justice which go beyond distribution of resources and towards equalisation of social relations. This implies that their 'negative aim' is not so much to eliminate the impact of brute luck on 'who gets what' but to end domination and oppression; their 'positive aim' is not so much to ensure a perfect distribution of resources but to create a society in which people stand in relations of equality to others (Anderson, 1999). Ending domination and oppression for the sake of creating a society of equals presupposes public acts of resistance. As Boaventura de Sousa Santos (2018: 97) argues:

> Although it is the existential basis for denouncing domination, unjust suffering, in itself, cannot spark resistance. What sparks resistance is a triple discovery: that the oppressor has weak spots; that there are paths no matter how narrow, to fight against oppression; and that there is some capacity to tread those paths. Herein lies the hope (the opening up of an opportunity) and the joy (the capacity to benefit from it) without which no resistance is possible.

Resistance is morally and politically justified on the grounds that inequality of social relations is objectionable not only because it reflects humiliating differences in status and power, inequality of opportunity and unfairness of political institutions and violation of equal concern (Scanlon, 2018) but also because it undermines social cohesion and social reproduction. To put it another way, no society can survive long-term unless shared institutions, including the state and global institutions ensure that social bonds are maintained through enforced non-ideal standards of social equality and respect to citizens.

2.2 Applying Non-Ideal Justice in Innovation

How does the idea of justice in non-ideal terms apply to innovation and technological change? As such, innovation is a human action. This kind of action is about novelty. As I have argued elsewhere:

> Whether it be doing something (a product or a process) new to the firm, new to the market or new to the world, or something old in new ways, the concept of innovation describes the restless efforts of human beings to provide novel solutions to problems and to transform their technical and socio-economic environment.
>
> (Papaioannou, 2018)

Innovation is not, of course, a new concept. It originates from the Greek word 'καινοτομία' that means 'doing something new'. The Latin verb 'innovave' also means to 'renew' something. Godin (2008) has argued that, as such, innovation is a political concept that aims to change existing conditions or the status quo. Sociologically, innovation implies change and evolution. Since the first industrial revolution in the 19th century, innovation has been focused on technical and technological change which had tremendous impact on global development. From industrial textiles and railways to medicines and information and communication technologies (ICTs), radical and incremental innovations have improved human well-being dramatically. According to Perez (2002: 1):

> Each technological revolution … is an explosion of new products, industries and infrastructures that gradually gives rise to a new techno-economic paradigm which guides entrepreneurs, managers investors and consumers, both in their individual decisions and in their interactions for the whole period of propagation of that set of technologies.

Certainly, the prominence of innovation in our lives in the 21st century is evident. Emerging technologies, ranging from artificial intelligence

(AI) and machine learning (ML) to the internet of things (IoT) and new life sciences such as gene editing, increasingly transform our productive capacities, health, and social relations.

Using computers for automated decision-making that is more effective than human intelligence and making interventions into human genome to combat genetic diseases have emerged as crucial milestones in the direction of the 21st century-technological innovation. These technologies are not value neutral. Rather they embody values and interests which are often in line with hegemonic, moral, and political narratives such as neo-liberalism, failing to meet the requirements of social justice (Papaioannou and Srinivas, 2019). For example, current automated machines, robots, and AI tend to impact unfairly on labour markets, displacing not only low-skilled jobs but also high-skilled services. There is growing empirical evidence that suggests the beneficiaries of accelerated innovation in the 21st century are just a few high-skilled workers whereas the losers are many (Zehavi and Bresnitz, 2017; Alden and Litan, 2017). In the developing world the impacts of automation might be even more negative than in the developed world since in the developing world there are more manual jobs to be lost through labour-substituting innovation than in the developed world. The World Bank (2019) estimation is for about 1.8 billion jobs to be threaten by emerging technologies in the developing world.

In addition to job losses due to AI applications in the global South, new phenomena of oppression and exploitation and coloniality have emerged. One of them is algorithmic oppression. According to Mohamed et al (2020: 666)

> Algorithmic oppression extends the unjust subordination of one social group and the privileging of another – maintained by a 'complex network of social restrictions' ranging from social norms, laws, institutional rules, implicit biases and stereotypes – through automated data driven and predictive systems.

Eubanks (2018) has documented several cases of automated inequality taking place not only in the global South but also in the global North. She has argued for dismantling what she called 'digital poorhouse' (i.e. digital barriers raised for poor and working-class people attempting to access shared material and relational resources) in countries such as the United States through politics of public action and campaigning against relational injustice.

Another phenomenon is that of algorithmic exploitation. According to Mohamed et al (2020) algorithmic exploitation considers the ways in which institutional actors and industries that surround algorithmic tools take advantage of often already marginalised people by unfair or unethical means for asymmetrical benefit of these industries. Examples include 'ghost workers' annotating large volumes of data and 'beta-testing' in neo-colonial exploitative settings (Mohamed et al, 2020). Finally, there is emerging algorithm coloniality in a number of AI systems. Mohamed et al (2020) recognise analogues of territorial and structural coloniality in digital technologies and propose the application of decolonial theory to AI. According to them 'Digital spaces – created by the Internet and increasingly networked systems and devices we use – form digital territories that, like physical spaces, have the propensity to become sites of extraction and exploitation, and thus, the sites of digital-territorial coloniality' (Mohamed et al, 2020: 665).

Colonial extractivism today even extends to the mining for data (Madianou, 2019). Within contemporary capitalism, there is a strong link between extractivism and colonianism in digital innovation. In a recent article, Madianou (2019) uses the term 'technocolonianism' to describe this link, focusing predominantly on the humanitarian sector. In her view:

> technocolonianism acknowledges that phenomena like displacement, migration, refugee camps, humanitarianism, and the development of digital technology itself are steeped in colonial relations of inequality. Technocolonianism shifts the attention to the constitutive role of data and digital innovation play in entrenching inequalities between refugees and humanitarian agencies and ultimately inequalities in the global context.

Such inequalities are not only material in terms of economic resources but predominantly relational in terms of domination, exploitation and oppression.

The potential outcome of technological innovation in the 21st century is predominantly unjust given that it leaves many people worst off from a relational perspective. Therefore, it requires attribution of political responsibility to individuals and institutions for changing the direction of innovation towards a more just outcome. I will return to the issue of direction of innovation in Chapter 5. For the time being, let me discuss in more detail the notion of justice in innovation.

In their well-known article 'Justice in the Diffusion of Innovation', Buchanan et al (2011) clearly defined justice in innovation as:

> the conformity of both the distribution of the fruits of the processes of innovation and of the character of the innovation process itself to the requirement of justice. Justice in innovation may require a pro-active stance: that is, it may be necessary to shape the innovation process in the name of justice, either to try to avoid the production of justice-degrading new technologies or to harness the innovation process for the purpose of promoting justice.

However, this definition still seems to conceive the requirements of justice in broad ideal terms, failing to encourage an empirical diagnosis of relational inequalities in the process of new knowledge generation and exploitation. Such inequalities range from marginalisation of certain types of knowledge and needs (e.g. indigenous knowledge, needs of Bottom of the Pyramid (BOP), etc.) to domination of multinational companies in global value chains (e.g. oppression of local producers, etc.) and the development of new methods for controlling research agendas (e.g. venture capital partnerships) by these companies (Foxon and Kanger, 2018). Current regulatory structures such as intellectual property rights (IPRs) promote unequal appropriation and commodification of new products and processes. These structures and inequalities are clearly unjust in virtue of our concern for securing equal relations in innovation. Imagined solutions to innovation inequalities constitute bottom-up requirements of justice. They include openness towards non-R&D generated knowledge, participation of marginalised groups in innovation processes, empowerment of local producers in global value chains, abolishment of certain IPR structures such as patents, elimination of power dynamics between advantaged societies in the global North and disadvantaged societies in the global South due to persistent coloniality, etc. After all, science and technology advance not only through high-tech R&D from inside labs but also through low-tech processes in sheds, garages, workshops and marginalised communities. The idea of justice in innovation applies in both processes. Whether high-tech or low-tech, innovation as such ought to promote a society of equal relations between people. For this to happen, structures which impact knowledge generation and exploitation for innovation as well as actions of innovators, regulators and publics ought to be evaluated from the perspective of relational justice.

Justice as such is a difficult subject area for theorisation. Buchanan et al (2011) recognise the following fact:

> Theorising about justice is afflicted ... with both disagreement and uncertainty. There is disagreement between consequentialists and deontologists, between proponents of 'positive' rights and libertarians, between egalitarians, prioritarians, and sufficientarians and among egalitarians as to what the 'currency' of justice is (well-being, opportunity for well-being, or resources). In addition, there is uncertainty as to how to move from a given theory's abstract, highest-level principles to lower-level principles with clearer implication for policies and institutions.

Yet, it might be suggested that disagreement and uncertainty are not necessarily issues for a non-ideal theory of justice in innovation. Since the latter considers egalitarian justice to be primarily relational, its currency can be multiple, ranging from well-being (e.g. capabilities) to resources (e.g. income), provided that it enables people involved in innovation (e.g. innovators, regulators, publics) to stand in relations of equality to one another. In addition, a non-ideal theory of justice in innovation does not need to be preoccupied with the question of how to move from highest-level principles to lower-level principles. Public actions for justice in innovation, at local and global levels, have already generated and articulated bottom-up principles with clear relational and institutional implications.

In my previous work on *Inclusive Innovation for Development* (2018: 80) I tried to formulate these principles as follows:

Equity: All persons are of equal moral worth and deserve to stand in relations of equality to one another in the process of innovation generation and distribution.

Recognition: All persons ought to be recognised and respected as equals in terms of their basic needs for innovation.

Participation: All persons are entitled to equal rights of participation in the innovation process of their societies.

The three principles of relational justice in innovation are in line with theories of justice focused on equal respect, recognition, capability, and ubuntu. All of them can be defended on non-ideal grounds. They are non-ideal principles of justice because everyone who follows them in his/her innovation context has an effective voice in their consideration and is able to agree to them without coercion. For innovation to be just, it must follow these principles enabling all to meet their needs. What people need in order to be in equal relations with others, to feel recognised and respected for their contribution to economy and society, and to equally participate in social and political processes, goes beyond material resources. In this sense, just innovation principles ought to be egalitarian, thus preventing people from entering superior-inferior relations in the social process of innovation. Phases of oppression, whether they be marginalisation, hierarchy, domination, or exploitation (Young, 1990), have no place in innovative communities of equals. Such communities are democratic in the sense that innovators, regulators, and users are not in relations of hierarchy with one another but in relations of equality. Relations of equality as such ought not to be influenced by naturally acquired talents and asymmetries of knowledge, material resources, opportunities, and capabilities. Rather, they ought to be based on social cooperation and the sharing of ideas and resources.

To borrow a phrase from Nozick (1974), if the innovation process of a society was wholly just, the principles of equity, recognition and participation would be reflected in every relation between innovator, regulator, and user. As a result, no innovative product and/or process would be exclusive of the interests and aspirations of low-income people. Non-ideal principles of justice in innovation embody imagined solutions to identified problems of knowledge hierarchies and power asymmetries in technological change, domination and oppression of local needs which never transform into effective demand for innovative products due to poverty and inequality. Historical evidence suggests that high-tech innovations which are not guided by these principles tend to face issues of legitimacy. Such issues are eventually addressed through public action and campaigning for just innovation.

In the first half of 21st century, public activists' claims for justice in innovation appear to be gathering momentum in both the global North and the global South. This is because advances in science and technology directly lead to relational and distributional concerns which are framed as concerns of justice in terms of non-ideal principles. Take for example the concerns of just distribution of health technologies such as innovative vaccines and drugs and medical devices to combat Covid-19. Such concerns are clearly reflected in the recent World Health Organisation (WHO) solidarity call to public action to

'… realise equitable global access to Covid-19 health technologies through pooling of knowledge, intellectual property and data' (WHO, 2020). Supported by global activists and campaigners such as Global Justice Now, Medecins Sans Frontiers (MSF), and Oxfam GB, as well as developing countries such as Costa Rica, the WHO's solidarity call to public action aims to prevent big pharmaceutical companies to profit from the pandemic to the detriment of equitable access to Covid-19 technologies. Framing this as a claim of justice in innovation, the WHO and public activists are now able to promote a vision of change according to non-ideal principles of equity, recognition and participation. According to Smith et al (2017: 166):

> Frames are seen as a fundamental part of the affirmation of collective identity, values, motivations and visions of change, and a reference point for action, as well as being shaped through action. Framing is understood to be a process negotiated among activists.

Pragmatically speaking, public activists and campaigners for justice in innovation call for better interaction between formal and informal actors and institutions and focus on localised needs and the equal diffusion of innovations within communities (Papaioannou, 2014; Foster & Heeks, 2013; Smith et al, 2010; Thomas et al, 2012). For example, People's Science Network in India has a membership of 700 thousand and focuses on local needs and aspirations, including health, education, and the environment. As Smith et al (2017: 52) observe:

> activists' practical confrontation with social and economic issues generated a rich plurality of knowledge. Whether highlighting and addressing the exclusions and inequities in existing grassroots innovation … or pointing to injustices in society, a figuring-out of issues through material projects proved both informative and expressive for participants. Movement initiatives and spaces permitted finer-grained and more richly textured forms of knowledge production as compared to, say, more rarefied analysis and argument in manifestos, reports and policy documents.

Activists and campaigners' demands for radical social and institutional changes increasingly undermine traditional and hierarchical innovation systems. Such changes involve conflict politics that constitutes the foundation of a non-ideal theory of justice in innovation. Through such politics, activists pave the way for a normative direction of innovation that is more transformative of people's lives and more consistent with the demands of justice. This direction does not only mean opening innovation to those who, up till now, have been excluded from use of the high- and low-tech products and processes that are crucial for their survival, but also constructing an entirely new set of equal social relations among the actors involved in the generation and diffusion of new technologies. This is of course not to say that public activists always enable socially just technologies. There are also cases in which public activists have blocked or opposed technologies with huge potential for social justice, e.g., genetically modified (GM) food technologies and medical application of genetic engineering technologies (gene therapy). In these cases, concerns were not so much about social inclusion but about risk and safety which eventually undermined public confidence and constrained technological innovation. Especially in the case of GM, deliberative exercises and the public debate with strong participation of activists, sent out the message that people were uneasy about these technologies and mistrusted both government and multinational companies (Gaskell, 2004).

2.3 Implications for Public Policy

What implications for public policy a theory of justice in innovation might have? To answer this question, we need to be aware of the historical fact that public policy very much depends on the kind of state and more specifically on the kind of public bureaucracy which produces it. I will discuss the role of the state in innovation extensively in Chapter 6. However, here, I would like to stress that until very recently, the notion of the state as a political institution that has a role to play in the generation of new knowledge and technologies was absent from the area of innovation studies. More than hundred years ago the founding father of this inter-disciplinary area, Joseph Schumpeter, clearly saw the interplay between politics and economics, influencing the ideas of Chris Freeman (1981, 1991) and Carlota Perez (2002) and other neo-Schumpeterian thinkers. However, for more than two decades (1990–2010), political notions such as the state had almost vanished from academic and policy debates on technological change and progress. This is partly because of the historical fact that politics and the state were attacked and increasingly dismantled during the peak of neo-liberalism in Western economies and partly because of the domination of innovation studies by liberal economists who were sceptical of the importance of politics for understanding economics. The latter is a discipline that has overwhelmingly focused on efficiency and growth, overlooking the distributional effects of innovation which are, by definition, political. That is to say, innovation can improve inclusion or exacerbate exclusion depending on the political framework within which it is generated and distributed.

In the early 2010s the relationship between innovation and politics begun to warm up again. It was when several innovation scholars and political scientists discovered that technological progress would not automatically lead to social progress and that the state was in fact behind almost all investments in radical technological revolutions, including the Internet and digital revolution. The return of the state in innovation was essentially confirmed in 2014 with the publication of Mazzucato's work on *The Entrepreneurial State: Debunking Public vs. Private Sector Myths*. This work follows a trend of state intervention theory and/or reaffirms the idea of strategic state that has been around for more than half century. Before Mazzucato, Schumpeter, Keynesian, neo-Keynesian and Marxist theorists, including Karl Polanyi and much later Fred Block, debunked the myth of self-regulating markets and stressed the crucial role of the state in economic growth. But Mazzucato goes further than them, arguing that the state is not a simple facilitator of economic growth. Rather, it should be understood as a key partner of the private sector when it comes to searching for growth and technological change. This partnership includes offering knowledge platforms, mobilising and empowering actors, and co-creating process and product innovations.

Mazzucato's argument clearly intends to move the current political and economic debate away from 'market failure' justifications. For example, during the peak of the pandemic in Spring 2020, the UK market failed to ensure sufficient availability of personal protection equipment (PPE) and medicines due to both de-industrialisation and outsourcing of manufacturing to emerging economies, e.g., China. This justified state intervention for emergency re-purposing of manufacturing in the UK. In the post-Covid era, such kind of justification might indeed encourage policies to fund basic research and infrastructure projects in order to deal with the unwillingness or inability of private firms to invest in economic and social recovery. However, they might not push the state to play a 'visionary strategic role' in the economy and society. For Mazzucato, that is precisely the problem with current economic theory that guides public policy. It is not inspiring enough of visionary state actions for innovation and development in the 21st century. The state needs to be entrepreneurial in order to engage in risk taking, shape markets and create a new vision (e.g. strengthening public health) that provides direction to innovation rather than just fixing market failures. Industrial policy of the entrepreneurial state should become the driving engine of technological innovations which can help accomplish grand missions, e.g., promoting green growth, eradicating poverty and reducing inequality in the post-Covid era.

However, state missions cannot be, by definition, just from a relational perspective. Mazzucato's entrepreneurial state can in fact take different forms (e.g. liberal, neo-liberal, libertarian states, authoritarian, socialist, welfare states, etc.). Each form includes legitimacy constraints and conditions which impact on social justice. This implies two things: first, some forms of the state (e.g. authoritarian, socialist, welfare states, etc.) might be legitimate to openly become more entrepreneurial than some other states (e.g. liberal, neo-liberal, libertarian states, etc.); second, entrepreneurial interventions of some forms of the state (especially neo-liberal or libertarian states) might not be sustained for a long time. These states are bound to be short-term 'institutional entrepreneurs' due to lack of legitimacy that arises as a result of their failing to maintain neutrality towards particular innovations and/or firms (i.e. picking up winners) or as a result of their failing to control the impact of these innovations on fundamental freedoms and individual rights (e.g. digital surveillance). To put it another way, the more neo-liberal or libertarian the entrepreneurial state becomes, the less polices for social justice.

Clearly, the mission-oriented policies of say neo-liberal or libertarian states would always be different from those of say welfare states in terms of social justice. For example, welfare states can justify policies for redistributing the benefits of innovation for as long as they are in power. Yet the issue of relational justice in innovation remains open. To address it, non-ideal public policy solutions are required. These might be implemented or tried on the ground in order to deal with relational injustices. Take for example technologies such as digital interactive maps and voice-activated personal assistants, facial recognition, activity predictors and surveillance systems. The point of equality in these technologies is not primarily about distributing them equally to all. Rather, it is about identifying relational inequalities because of algorithmic oppression, exploitation and coloniality which affect disproportionately minorities and marginalised groups (e.g. failure of commercial face detection systems to notice dark-skinned faces) or because of data bias towards the poor (e.g. failure of an algorithmic decision system to identify children at risk for abuse in wealthy families, and instead overwhelmingly focusing on poor families which receive public assistance). Through such identification, innovation policy can ensure processes and products of ML and AI take on board the interests and aspirations of everyone in innovative communities of equals. To do so, innovation policy can implement measures ranging from distribution of resources to minorities and marginalised groups to development of conditions for their involvement in the shaping and testing of these technologies. I will return to the policy challenge of emerging technologies in Chapter 4.

2.4 Concluding Remarks

This chapter has distinguished between an ideal and non-ideal justice in innovation. It has defended the latter as a pragmatic approach to delivering relational just outcomes of innovation. The principles of non-ideal justice in innovation emerge from the bottom-up through every day public action and campaigning. This has implications for public policy that needs to respond to claims and complaints for relational injustice in the processes of knowledge generation and exploitation.

Relational injustice is about asymmetries of knowledge and inequalities of resources and capabilities which impact negatively on equality between innovators, regulators, and publics. The requirement here is for these relational inequalities to be addressed. However, it is clear that some asymmetries and inequalities are personal choices. Thus, they don't create oppressive or exclusive relations between innovators, regulators, and publics.

From a non-ideal perspective, a relational justice in innovation ought to allow legitimate incentives for innovative entrepreneurship and freedom. For this reason, it needs to evaluate which claims of injustice impact on relations of different people involved in processes of knowledge generation and exploitation. If such claims turn to be individual choices which don't reduce inequality of relations, then they should be allowed to function as incentives for generating new technologies and processes to respond to needs.

3 Justice and Development

In the preceding chapter, I suggested that when it comes to innovation, the idea of justice we should defend is both non-ideal and relational. But what about the idea of development that is impacted by innovation? What is the relationship between (a non-ideal) justice and development? Before attempting to answer these questions, I would like to reflect on the following personal experience. When I began writing the basic outline of this chapter it was the second half of the year 2022. During that time, I received a message on my mobile phone that reminded me I should book my appointment for my fourth Covid-19 vaccination. Other people had probably received a similar message if they were of a certain age and lived in the United Kingdom (UK) or another country of the so-called global North (e.g. European countries, the United States (US), Canada, etc.). However, if they lived in a developing country of the global South, it would be perfectly possible that they had received none of these messages. For example, in countries such as Burundi and the Democratic Republic of Congo, the rate of vaccination in September 2022 was just under 5 doses per 100 people. This fact might lead to the conclusion that people in the global North were, after all, better protected against Covid-19 than people in the global South thanks to their power in determining the diffusion of technological innovation such as Covid-19 vaccines. Yet data suggests that during the earliest stages of the pandemic, highly unequal countries of the global North, including the US, the UK, Italy, and Spain, were the worst-hit in total mortalities comparing to more equal countries of the global South (IPP, 2020).

Unequal relations in terms of accessing and using new technologies is of course a crucial feature of injustice between and within countries.

DOI: 10.4324/9781003652083-4

The Covid-19 pandemic is now over, and we have the knowledge and the technologies to combat it. This is substantial progress. Yet from a non-ideal justice perspective, the issue remains: some countries (including Burundi and the Democratic Republic of Congo) and some disadvantaged socioeconomic groups in both global South and global North do not relate equally in terms of securing the required knowledge and technology to combat diseases. As a result of it, they continue to face avoidable loss of lives and destruction of livelihoods. This is a huge concern for non-ideal justice in innovation. More importantly, it has serious implications for global development. To put it another way, similarly to innovation, the relationship between non-ideal justice and development is crucial for delivering change that takes on board the interests of everyone.

This chapter is focused on innovation justice and development contradictions (e.g. on the one hand, generation of innovative health technologies against Covid-19 and on the other unequal access to these technologies between and within countries). It argues that to understand normative and analytical intervention, we need the critical lenses of development theory. Key concerns of this theory are: power relations; agency; scale; and history. Approaches to development as a planned process (i.e. structuralism, dependency theory, interventionism) address each of these concerns differently than approaches to development as an unplanned process (i.e. liberalism, neo-liberalism, modernisation theory) and post-development (i.e. people-centred development, post-development, alternative development). A non-ideal theory of justice in innovation needs to be complemented with development theory so that it becomes aware of the role of power relations, agency, scale, and history in creating injustice in production and distribution of new technologies.

But what do we actually mean by development? Like innovation, development as such can be simply defined as a process of change. For example, responding to the Covid-19 pandemic through social adaptation and technological innovation is one such change. Some authors insist that development is about 'good change' (Chambers, 2017). However, as Thomas (2021: 48) points out:

> the two words 'good change' combine quite different ideas. Good implies a vision of desirable things and circumstances ('wellbeing for all') something to aim at … Meanwhile, change is not in itself a normative concept, and may apply to social processes that are

far from benign, may entail disruption and may not be possible to direct.

Although the gap between normativity (what ought to be) and analytical fact (what is) in development studies is in essence a gap between theory and practice, Thomas is right to argue that in the long run the concept of development implies improvement of living standards, health, and human capabilities. To put it another way, the positive meaning of this concept is synonymous with progress at all aspects of human life and the environment. In several respects, such progress is determined by technological innovation that is also about change and improvement of the ways we do things. If technological innovation is unjust from a non-ideal and relational perspective, then development is likely to be less progressive and more regressive from the point of view of non-ideal justice.

Certainly, like any other process of social change, including innovation, development is heavily contested. This is not only because within the current economic system of innovative capitalism, change creates winners and losers (e.g. those who have access to technological innovation such as vaccines and other health technologies against diseases and those who do not) but also because it provokes heated debates and conflicts over the normative direction of social and technological change, i.e., what ought to change. Various approaches to development reflect these normative and analytical conflicts about the nature of innovation and development practice, the political and policy debates in the global North and global South, the argument of civil society activists, campaigners for development and non-governmental organisations (NGOs).

The purpose of this chapter is to make sense of the relation between justice and development (e.g. increasing the rate of Covid-19 vaccinations per 100 people in the global South) by briefly reviewing some key theoretical approaches. Such approaches are generalised explanations of how development does and ought to occur so that it is socially just and improves the lives of people. In what follows, I examine how influential key approaches to development have been for building just institutions and guiding policies and practices of social and technological change. Section 3.2 will suggest that major developmental interventions such as the establishment of post-World War II Bretton Woods institutions of World Bank (WB) and the International Monetary Fund (IMF) in 1944 are 'big D' development taking pace within the broader context of 'little d' development of global capitalism. This section will show that both types of development involve unjust social relations of power, agency, scale and history. Section 3.3 will discuss development as a planned process, emphasising three related theories: structuralism; dependency theory and interventionism. Section 3.4 will analyse development as an unplanned and evolutionary process, focusing on three related theories: liberalism, neo-liberalism and modernisation theory. Section 3.5 will move on to post-development approaches, discussing three related theories: people-centred; alternative development; and post-colonial development. Throughout this chapter I will make references to thinkers from both the global North and the global South. This is crucial for theorising justice and development in decolonial terms. Decolonisation requires questioning the Eurocentric terms of justice, progress, and development, foregrounding indigenous and marginalised theories of development.

3.1 The Notion of Development

The notion of development as change and/or progress goes back to the philosophers of the Enlightenment in the 17th century. In fact, such philosophers can be found in both the global North (e.g. Descartes, Locke, Montesquieu, etc.) and global South (e.g. Yacob, Amo, etc.). The scientific and philosophical advances of that historical time were founded upon the concept of human reason which was regarded as conducive to progress of individuals and their societies. In this sense, the notion of development in relation to societies implies change to something fairer and more advanced (Harriss, 2014) for which technological innovation is key. Thinking about development represents an effort to understand and conceptualise this process of '… pervasive, continuous social change to which human actors attribute particular meaning and value – and which they believe, in some sense and to a varying extent, they may be able to influence' (Hettne, 2009: 8).

Certainly, the simplest way to understand 'advance' or 'progress' is in terms of increasing wealth and economic prosperity through the success of new technologies in the liberal economic market. This understanding of innovation-driven growth and development dominated policy and practice since 1945. Development has been measured as innovation-driven growth of wealth and economic prosperity using indicators such as the so-called gross domestic product

(GDP). However, these indicators tend to ignore increasing relational inequalities in terms of domination, oppression and exploitation of people and groups. To put it another way, economic advance and progress does not necessarily imply advance and progress in terms of non-ideal justice. As has been argued so far, non-ideal justice is above all relational, even though often determined by economic inequality.

The birth and expansion of industrial capitalism as a global system in the 19th and 20th centuries has led to the theorising of development as a synonymous to innovation-driven economic growth. For example, development economics was set up as an academic discipline to provide theoretical modelling and empirical analysis of how innovation-driven economic growth comes about and then trickles down to individuals and social groups (Charles and Williams, 2001). Not surprisingly, this one-dimensional theorising of development and innovation received criticism from thinkers such as Amartya Sen who argued that economic productivity and growth, thanks to proliferation of new technologies, have value only if they enable us to be and do what we chose. For Sen (1999) development ought to be about expansion of individual freedom and just distribution of capabilities through the removal of various types of natural and social obstacles that leave people with little choice and little opportunity for exercising agency. Recall this chapter's opening discussion of Covid-19. Diseases such as Covid-19 are obstacle to just development. These obstacles can be removed through equalising capabilities for accessing and using innovative health technologies. Such equalisation implies a more just society in terms of how people relate to certain technologies (especially in health, education, etc.) and to each other (as social and political beings).

The intrinsic dynamism of capitalism and its tendency to build on itself and grow from within due to restless technological innovation has been regarded by Hart (2001) as 'little d' development. This immanent and unplanned development process is differentiated from the intentional and politically planned development. The latter is regarded by Hart (Hart, 2001) as 'big D' development and refers to the US led project of post-World War II intervention in the 'third world' that emerged in the context of decolonisation.

It is well known that the inauguration of the new era of development took place on the 20th of January 1949 when Harry Truman became President of the US and declared that

> We must embark on a bold new program for making the benefits of our scientific advances and industrial progress available for the improvement and growth of underdeveloped areas. The old imperialism – exploitation for foreign profit – has no placed in our plans. What we envisage is a program of development based on the concepts of democratic fair dealing.
>
> (Esteva, 1992: 6)

For many development theorists, this statement summarises the main principles of the 20th-century decolonial development, including freedom, democracy, and fairness. However, reflecting on this statement more critically, Langdon (2013) points out that, in fact, what Truman attempts to do is consolidate the post-World War II US technological and economic hegemony in a rather patronising way. He assumes the role of the US and other powerful countries of the global North as defenders of freedom and democracy around the world. As Rist (2002) points out, Truman's call for decolonisation and development did not necessarily mean be free from the advanced countries but rather meant be like the advanced countries. The whole idea of 'catching up' of developing countries with advanced countries was based on Trumann's speech. Nonetheless, as Langdon (2013) stresses, Truman's speech can also be interpreted as a call for decolonisation. There is a link between the emergence of development and decolonisation (Kothari, 2005). For example, the original purpose of 'Big D' development of Bretton Woods institutions of the WB and the IMF was to assist new countries emerging from the decolonisation process and old countries emerging from World War II to create a dynamic economic system through cooperation in many areas, including technological innovation.

3.2 Understanding Development

Theorising development started much earlier than the middle of the 20th century. Indeed, as Harriss (2014: 7) suggest:

> we may look for the roots of contemporary development theories in the work of classical economists such as Adam Smith, in that of Marx and Engels, or in that of Friedrich List, who, writing in the 1840s, … advocated state intervention to ensure national prosperity.

Other early theories of development also emerged in the global South, notably India where thinkers such as Dadabhai Naoroji and R. C. Dutt argued that the cause of India's underdevelopment was the colonial rule. According to Harriss (Harriss, 2014) these arguments '... influenced the later formulation of "dependency theory" largely through the more direct influence of Paul Baran's *The Political Economy of Growth*' (1957). In Section 3.4, I will discuss the dependency theory in more detail.

For the time being, it is worth mentioning that theorists of development came from different parts of the world: West, East, South, and North. For example, Harriss (2014) reminds us that a number of remarkable scholars came from Russia or Eastern Europe. They include Alexander Gerschenkron (born in Odessa), Albert Hirschman (born in Berlin), Hans Singer (a German Jew), and Karl Polanyi and Friedrich Hayek (both born in Vienna). Theorists from the South include: Arthur Lewis (born in the Caribbean) and Raul Prebisch (born in Argentina). The emergence of development theorists in different parts of the world demonstrates the global nature of processes of social, economic and technological change and the need for understanding them as global development phenomena.

All scholars listed above, one way or another, made significant contributions to explaining innovation-driven global development and effectively address four interrelated concerns: power relations, agency, scale, and history. These four concerns can be understood as a basic framework within which we can make sense of development phenomena in relation to justice and innovation. In a non-ideal world, power relations, agency, scale and history lie behind the just or unjust way people relate to one another when it comes to innovation. For example, exclusion of certain publics from new technologies and new phenomena of digital colonialism are due to power relations between global North and global South.

Power Relations

Development and innovation phenomena involve power relations which are often unjust due to dominant and oppressive control. Recall the case of unequal rate of Covid-19 vaccination from the opening paragraph of this chapter. One might argue that the ability of countries such as the US, the UK, and the EU to control the innovative production and supply of vaccines had a negative impact on other countries' response to the pandemic in both global North and global South. This is an unequal relationship of power between strong and weak countries in terms of controlling economic resources, technology, and institutions. Such inequality cannot be possibly justified from the point of view of relational justice.

Although different theorists of innovation and development from Marx to Hayek disagree on the meaning of power, they all recognise its relational nature and its importance for agents and structures of innovation and development to determine the direction of social and political change. For example, Marx (2000) sees the state as a political superstructure that imposes its power on society. For him progress is to achieve the subordination of the former to the latter. In contrast, Hayek sees the market as a spontaneous order that has the just power to improve the lives of individuals, maximising their freedom (Hayek, 1960).

Agency

As has been already implied, states and markets are often regarded as powerful institutional (super)structures of both innovation and development. This is because they consist of rules and resources which influence processes and outcomes of technological and social change. For example, for Marx, the constant innovation and material resources within capitalism constitute the structural base that determines, or controls change in superstructure, including politics and culture (McLellan, 1977). However, social theory has showed that Marx is not necessarily correct in attributing so much power to social and economic structures. Individuals and social groups (innovators, regulators and publics) are also powerful agents of change, especially towards social justice. They have the capacity to make choices and act independently of unjust structural constrains. As has been already implied, activism as such is crucial for achieving justice in innovation and development. As Sriskandarajah (2024) shows in his recent book *Power to People*, activism and social movements can influence the direction of development and innovation towards more just relational outcomes in both the global North and global South. According to him,

> there is no shortage of ideas for improving the way that political institutions work, changing the way our economics are organised,

> improving how global decisions are made and securing our digital futures.
>
> (Sriskandarajah, 2024: 294)

Of course, discussions over the primacy of either structure or agency have dominated sociological theories and development studies for a long time. This is because such theories try to address the question of what causes social phenomena such as development to occur. The solution to this problem of structure-agency dualism has been provided by Giddens (1984) who argued that social phenomena should be understood in terms of both agency and structure. His theory of the so-called structuration argues that people's activities have institutional embeddedness. Therefore, agency and structure cannot be empirically separated. The dualism is valid only in theoretical and analytical terms.

Individuals and groups can act together as agents of innovation and development, recognising and promoting their own interests. Such non-state agents of innovation and development change have gained high profile towards the end of the 20th century and the beginning of the 21st century. They include: international bodies; multinational companies; non-government organisations (NGOs); social movements; and various civil society groups. In a recent work, Green and Kirk (2021) classify these groups of innovation and development agents into three overarching categories: state, societal, and international actors, and organisations. These broad categories can be seen in parallel to our more specific categories of innovators, regulators and publics. However, the crucial point to keep in mind is that agents of innovation and development interact with one another in various ways and/or build coalitions and structures towards achieving specific visions or goals of development. For example, historical campaigns such as the *Jubilee 2000 Dept Cancelation* and the *Make Poverty History* at the dawn of the 21st century involved NGOs, trade unions, charities, and faith groups (Papaioannou et al, 2009) signalling the importance of societal and international actors for influencing the direction of development in the new millennium. More recently the so-called Occupy movement (2011) and the Back Lives Matter (2013) movement involved community organisations and individuals who used new technologies and social media to coordinate their activism.

Scale

Power relations and agency take place at different scales, including household, local community, sub-national regional level, national, international, and global scales. Traditional innovation and development studies tended to prioritise national and international scales of comparative analysis given the post-World War II focus on economic growth and GDP indicators. The most debated models of innovation and development at that scale were the US and the Soviet Union (USSR). These models put forward competing visions and indicators of just technological and social progress for other countries to follow. One was about equal economic freedom or liberty (US) and the other was about material equality (USSR). Structuralist and liberal theories of development have emerged from within this cold war context. However, both have been criticised for overlooking processes of change and their impact on the lives of individuals and households.

Specifically, as has been already mentioned in chapter 1, Sen's relational justice theory of capabilities '… concentrates on our capability to achieve valuable functions that make up our lives and more generally our freedom to promote objectives we have reasons to value' (Sen, 1999: xi). Sen's theory implies moving from concerns about economic growth to concerns about just improvement of the lives of poor people. Theories of people-centred and alternative development emerged from this line of criticism. They enabled comparisons not only between countries but also within countries. Such comparisons advanced development studies from their preoccupation with how the South would emulate the North and become developed to how the North/South boundary become blurred. Thus, Horner and Hulme (2019) argue for the need to go beyond international development considered as a binary between rich North and poor South, and to move towards a more holistic global development where the global South remains a key focus, but not necessarily an exclusive focus. This is a need for moving scales to understand innovation and development change in the world. Although the argument of Horner and Hulme has been challenged by other development scholars such as Fischer (2019), reaffirming the classical traditions of development studies, it is certain that the scale of development is not static but evolves along with historical change.

History

In 1944, Karl Polanyi, an Austro-Hungarian economic anthropologist, began his infamous book *The Great Transformation* by recognising the collapse of the 19th-century civilisation and trying to explain the political and economic causes of this historical event as well as the great transformation which it ushered in. In his theory, the 19th-century implementation of the idea of self-regulating market as a driver of development led to prioritisation of economic interests over social concerns and eventually gave rise to a counter movement and brought about the great transformation of Western societies.

Seventy-seven years later, in 2021, Harriss reconstructed Polanyi's arguments, placing history in the centre of his analysis. According to him:

> History does not repeat itself but for some observers of the Trump phenomenon in the United States, the mounting influence of right-wing political movements such as the Front National in France or Alternative fur Deutschland in Germany and the success of political 'strong men' elsewhere in the world – Viktor Orban in Hungary, Recep Erdogan in Turkey, Narenda Modi in India – carry echoes of the 1930s.
>
> (Harriss, 2021: 564)

If we add to these trends of history, the ongoing trade war between the US and the rest of the World, including China and India, the UK's exit from the EU (BREXIT), the re-emergence of nationalism through the Covid-19 pandemic, the 2022 war in Ukraine, the 2023 war in Middle East, the election of far-right in Italy and the re-election of Trump in the US, we can realise that this decade is essentially a decade of historical change for the world or indeed, as Harriss (2021) observes, of another great transformation. The latter, as many innovation and development theorists note, is following the previous decades' failure of neo-liberalism and the related Washington consensus to secure prosperity for all. Historically, neo-liberalism dismantled the post-World War II Bretton Woods system of fixed exchange rates and capital movement controls, creating a global landscape of multinational innovative corporations which could make huge profits avoiding taxation. As Harriss (2021: 570) points out:

> Neo-liberalism has succeeded, all too well, in restoring the class power of those who hold assets. Inequality has soared across most of the world.

Unjust inequality and the lack of concern for the poor was clearly reflected in the 2008 financial crisis and the subsequent austerity policies in countries such as Greece which inflicted further pain and suffering to the most vulnerable. Thinking of development and innovation as processes of history enables us to search for the countermovement to unjust market fundamentalism. Whether we look at the Occupy movement in Wall Street or the Extinction Rebellion movement in the streets of central London, it is clear that there is a countermovement, putting forward claims of non-ideal relational justice in innovation and development.

3.3 Development as a Planned Process

Some approaches to innovation and development have emphasised the importance of power and history while others have insisted on the primacy of agency and scale. Earlier in the chapter I touched upon the notion of 'big D' development that has been used to describe the intentional and rationally planned intervention in the post-World War II development process. Several 'big D' approaches emerged in the 1950s and the 1960s theorising the powerful role of state planning in different scales of economic development (especially through industrialisation) and market regulation. The most influential of these approaches are: structuralism; dependency theory; and interventionism. Each of them is underpinned by specific theoretical position on social justice.

Structuralism

This approach is concerned with the underlying social and economic structures of innovation and development. Unless changes in these structures occur, neither industrialisation nor equalisation of relations and resources can be achieved. Theorists such as Gerschenham (1962), a Russian-born American economic historian, reflected on the advanced and backward economies, emphasising the centrality of both capital and state intervention in closing technological and industrialisation gaps. In his view, the greater the backwardness, the more powerful intervention is necessary in the market structure. The objective of structuralism is innovation-driven economic growth that is broadly fair and less exploitative. The main structure for that is the state. Using more inclusive macroeconomic policies and central planning, the state could accelerate capital accumulation and industrialisation. This, for example, was the hope of 'new' states in Africa such as Uganda and Zimbabwe in the 1950s and 1960s given that they had inherited structuralist economies at independence from colonial powers. However, as Brett (2009: 202) notes:

> subsequent political and economic failures produced radical institutional change, involving shifts from democracy to authoritarianism and back again, and from structuralism to neo-liberalism.

Another key policy of structuralism at the time was import substitution industrialisation (ISI). Theorists such as the Argentine economist Raul Prebish (1950) and the German-born British development economist Hans Singer (1964) advanced the argument that international markets lead to great inequality between innovative industrialised economies (what Prebish called 'core') and non-industrialised, commodity producers (what Prebisch called 'periphery'). This inequality cannot be possibly justified. Therefore, the state in non-industrialised countries needs to play active role in developing domestic markets and subsidising innovative industries. Latin American countries and India in the 1960s and 1970s pursued such Import Substitution Industrialisation (ISI) policies. The downside of this strategy was neglect for agricultural development and reforms for land redistribution.

However, following the Covid-19 pandemic and the war in Ukraine in 2022 there are increasing voices in support of ISI in specific areas such as health technologies, food, and energy. Milanovic (2022), for example, predicts that Russia might pursue ISI as a way of dealing with the sanctions of Western countries for the war in Ukraine. As such ISI is based on the protection of domestic infant industries through tariffs, import quotas and subsidies to those industries. Evidence suggests that the so-called BRICS (Brazil, Russia, India, China, and South Africa) improved their economic performance through ISI policies. Specifically, using data from the WB Development Indicators from 1960 to 2016 in econometric estimations, Adewale (2017) argues that ISI policy helped to catalyse the industrialisation process of BRICS and thereby become convergent in the short run. In April 2025, the freshly re-elected Trump administration in the US imposed tariffs on goods coming to the country from almost all over the world. Although the impact of this policy on economic performance is still unclear, it can potentially re-activate ISI in many other countries across the globe.

Dependency Theory

Prebisch's work in the Economic Commission for Latin America (ECLA) and especially his argument about the relationship between core and periphery in international political economy very much influenced critiques of unjust market-based innovation and development and enabled the formulation of dependency theory. The latter emerged in the 1960s through the writings of German-American sociologist and economic historian Andre Cunder Frank, especially his *Capitalism and Underdevelopment in Latin America* (1967). Dependency theory was further advanced through the work of Brazilian Fernando Henrique Cardoso and the Chilean Enzo Faletto titled *Dependency and Development in Latin America.* Dependency theory emphasises the determinant role of historical trajectories in development and innovation. These trajectories are predominantly unfair for countries in the periphery of capitalism, e.g., former colonies.

Frank argues that underdevelopment and injustice are indeed a historical product of the past and present economic relations between underdeveloped (dependent) satellite countries and the developed (core) metropolitan countries. Although this argument received criticism from other Latin American theorists such as Palma (1978) for its rather mechanical analysis, it was advanced further by Cardoso and Faletto. However, the latter theorists accept that there may be various forms historical dependency as well as spaces for agency within international political economy. In other words, economic progress and change of social practices and institutions are still possible through policies such as ISI. Even in situations of historical dependency there are innovation and development alternatives available to countries. What is important is the power of the state in supporting these alternatives and changing the historical trajectory of innovation and development.

Interventionism

Critiques of structuralism and growth theories of development gathered momentum at the beginning of 1970s. According to Harriss (2014: 19):

> the experience of the developing countries, too, began to reveal the limitations of that orthodoxy. The many countries that had tried to plan industrial development behind protective trade barriers had begun to experience great difficulties in continuing to finance their investments (as was the case in India) and the industries that has been set up were generally run very inefficiently.

The other side of this coin of criticism was that innovation-driven economic growth had failed to reduce poverty and create better circumstances of social justice. During the 1990s the focus of development theory shifted from growth to the problem of reducing poverty through political intervention. The so-called interventionary approach to development combines both structuralist (state-led) and neo-liberal (market-led) policies to generate and fairly redistribute innovation-led growth at different scales. The rationale behind this is that both markets and states are important to development and therefore need not to fail but instead operate well in harmony, contributing to just outcomes for everyone.

Interventionism was very much reflected in the important debate about the 'Third Way' politics of the UK Labour government (1997–2010) and Bill Clinton's presidency of the US (1993–2001) as well as the innovation policies of developmental states of East Asia, e.g., South Korea, Hong Kong, Singapore, Taiwan, etc. Scholars such as Amsden (1989) and Wade (1990) had demonstrated that East Asian governments intervened extensively by picking up industrial winners and made selective use of trade restrictions. At the same time, they pursued policies of economic growth redistribution. As Harriss (2014: 26) points out 'They were regimes that combined carrots and sticks with regard to labour, ensuring labour discipline but also that labour benefited from economic growth'.

In 1997, the WB recognised that economic, social, and sustainable development is impossible without an effective state that is able to facilitate industrial development and complement markets (World Bank, 1997). More recently interventionism has become fashionable among academics and policymakers. Thus, it has been defended by a number of innovation and development theorists (Mazzucato, 2014, 2016; Perez, 2016; Schot and Steinmueller, 2016; Block and Keller, 2011) who argue that never more than today, it is necessary to rethink the state's entrepreneurial role in society and welfare. These theorists provide justification for the existence of a powerful political state not only as a set of institutions that intervenes to correct and protect markets but also as an institutional entity capable of creation of markets in risky areas of knowledge and technology for the sake of justice and development. I will come back to the entrepreneurial state arguments in Chapters 5 and 6 of this book.

3.4 Development as an Unplanned Process

In Section 3.2 of this chapter, I touched upon the notion of 'little d' development that is used to describe the immanent and rather unplanned and evolutionary development of capitalism through market forces. This process of development is generated through the unintended consequences of economic agency. Three approaches are well known for emphasising this kind of agency in development: liberalism; neo-liberalism and modernisation Theory. All three imply that social justice cannot be possibly achieved through the state but instead can come about spontaneously though the market. It is the latter that defines relations between people in innovation and development within liberal societies. Such relations are by definition unequal given the freedom of each individual to act in the market according to their plans and expectations.

Liberalism

Liberalism can be thought as the opposite of structuralism, treating the market as a self-regulating and evolutionary mechanism that promotes individual freedom through economic agency, e.g., exchanging privately owned goods and services. Some liberals derive their arguments from Scottish economists of the 18th century such as Adam Smith (1759/1976) and French physiocrats such as Anne-Robert Turgot (1750/1973). Both thinkers saw the economy as an autonomous system, opposing mercantilist regulation and suggesting free trade as a pathway to the 'wealth of nations'.

At the same time, classical liberals were deeply concerned about the unjust concentration of wealth in the hands of a very small group of individuals. Therefore, they justified limited state intervention for redistributing wealth to those perceived as disadvantaged. In Smith's *Theory of Moral Sentiments* (1759/2010) this justification is constructed through the moral sentiment of 'sympathy' and the theoretical device of 'impartial spectator'. The argument goes like this: the impartial spectator observes the market society and sympathises with the undeserved disadvantages of poor people, providing good reasons for intervention to rectify the injustice.

Markets and trade had to be innovative to increase total production in order for government to use it for development. Smith and Turgot provided the core features of the evolutionist modernisation paradigm in the Enlightenment. According to Hettne (2009: 41) this was

> in principle applicable even to backward or non-civilised areas. However, for Smith it was possible that some societies remained in a 'barbarous and uncivilised state'.

What Smith and Turgot had in mind here were the English and French colonies. The Enlightenment discourse did not directly challenge colonialism of the 18th and 19th centuries. Rather it focused on the values of emerging market society within the organised system of nation states called Westphalia. This is where liberalism and the modern development theory were to be founded. Such foundations remain open to questions from a relational justice perspective. Neither liberalism nor modern development theory have ever evaluated colonialism from a relational justice perspective.

Neo-liberalism

Neo-liberalism is defined as a reconstruction of 18th- and 19th-century ideas about economic liberalism. This approach also emphasises the unintended consequence of economic agency. It was theorised by Friedrich von Hayek (1960) at the London School of Economics and Milton Friedman (2017) at the University of Chicago. As Harvey points out, what started as a theory of minority group of liberal economists became a dominant approach of innovation and development policy and practice.

Neo-liberalism was historically championed by Prime Minister Margaret Thatcher in the UK and President Ronald Reagan in the US in the 1980s. According to Harvey (2005: 2) neo-liberalism:

> is a theory of political economic practices that proposes that human well-being can be best advanced by liberating individual entrepreneurial freedoms and skills within an institutional framework characterised by strong private property and free trade.

The main difference between neo-liberalism and classical liberalism is the former's indifference about the concentration of innovation-led economic growth and wealth in private hands and the need for some redistribution of resources. Thus, for example, Hayek rejects the notion of social justice altogether. In the second volume of his *Law Legislation and Liberty*, Hayek (1982) calls social justice as a 'mirage' that cannot be realised in practice. This implies that for him, neither equality of relations nor equality of resources is possible. No matter whether the terms of justice are ideal or non-ideal, equality contradicts freedom.

The development context in which neo-liberalism came about in the 20th century was different from that of the 19th century. According to Harriss (2014: 23):

> In the history of international development two events of great importance took place in the 1970s: first, the decision by the Organisation of Petroleum Counties (OPEC) to raise oil prices after the Arab-Israel war of 1973; second the so-called 'Volcher shock' of October 1979.

The first event increased the revenues of oil-producing countries, enabling them to provide easy credit to developing countries (i.e. petrodollars). The second event increased interest rates, causing major departmental crisis to countries which received credit in petrodollars. In this context, international development institutions such as the IMF and the WB applied neo-liberalism as their guiding doctrine towards assisting with rescheduling debts of developing countries, e.g., Mexico. These institutions required structural adjustment programmes, involving liberalisation of trade, deregulation of the market and privatisation of industries. This is what came to be regarded as Washington Consensus of the 1980s and as Harriss (2021: 570) observes:

> even though it came to be recognised that these programmes generally failed to restore economic growth, the three principles [liberalisation, deregulation and privatisation] have remained part of widely accepted common sense about economic policy across the world.

Indeed, a number of governments in both the global North (e.g. the UK, the EU, Japan, etc.) and the global South (e.g. South Africa,

Brazil, India, etc.) still pursue neo-liberal polices of liberalisation, deregulation and privatisation in the 21st century.

Modernisation

The approach to development as a process of modernisation took place in between liberalism and neo-liberalism in the 1950s and 1960s. According to this approach, developing countries should follow the historical footsteps of the liberal West. According to Eisenstadt (1966: 1):

> Historically, modernisation is the process of change towards those types of social, economic and political systems that have developed in Western Europe and North America from the seventeenth century to the eighteenth and have spread to other European countries and in the nineteenth and twentieth centuries to the South American and African continents.

This approach to development was very much reflected in Walt Rostow's infamous theory of the historical stages of economic growth (1960):

1. Traditional society characterised by subsistence farming.
2. Preconditions for take-off in terms of beginning to develop manufacturing industry.
3. Take off in terms of urbanisation and industrialisation.
4. Drive to maturity, diversifying industry and investing in infrastructure.
5. Age of high mass consumption in terms of mass production feeding consumer demand.

In the context of the Cold War, Rostow's theory was very influential among liberal and right-wing policy circles. Modernisation meant liberal transformation of many aspects of economic and social life through industrialisation. For Rostow, capitalism and economic liberalism were inseparable from modernisation and industrialisation. This also implies the link between modernisation and liberal democracy as a political form that '… allows for "freedom" in electing representatives to much "freedom" in the market' (Thomas, 2021: 59). Although history does not demonstrate this link in all cases of development (e.g.

East Asian countries), advocates of liberalism insist that a combination of capitalist industrialisation and liberal democracy is the only pathway to development (Fukuyama, 1995; Thomas, 2021).

3.5 Post-Development Approaches

Notions of innovation and development as planned and unplanned processes of (just or unjust) change came into crisis in the end of the 20th century due to their failure to accelerate growth and create conditions for socially just distribution of wealth. In addition, many African and other countries were experiencing civil war and violence Harriss (2021).

Both structuralism and liberalism can be regarded as mainstream approaches to development which insist on capital accumulation and industrialisation, proposing to address problems such as poverty and inequality through adjusted growth policies and/or SDGs which require state intervention. Their proposals are in contradistinction to relational justice that requires investigation of claims of oppression, domination, paternalism and exploitation independently of their economic basis. It might be said that post development approaches are direct reactions to these mainstream structuralist and liberal proposals for economic and social change. Such approaches emphasise the importance of agency and scale and include: people-centred development; post development; and alternative development. All three post-development approaches promote the idea of relational justice in innovation and development through bottom-up activism.

People-Centred Development

This approach to development is highly critical of innovation led economic growth proposals, focusing instead on human development. The latter includes policies for redistribution of wealth, improvement of education and skills, human health and other human needs. Since the 1990s the UNDP has championed the people-centred approach to development, shifting from economic resource indicators of production, e.g., GDP to social relational indicators of well-being and human capabilities for maximising freedom. Dudley Seers (1969) pioneered this approach suggesting that the aim of development is to enable people to realise their potential of human personality. In his view, six conditions are crucial to achieve:

1 The capacity to obtain food and other basic necessities for human life
2 The ability to find a job
3 The achievement of equality in social relations
4 The opportunity to participate in politics and government
5 The belonging to an independent nation
6 The provision of adequate education

Seers' conditions are clear critique of innovation led economic growth as a measuring standard of successful development. They indicate a third pathway to development based on self-sufficiency in basic food, low technology, non-competition culture, etc. According to Escobar (2019: 395) 'Seers' framework resembled positions advocated by radical Third World intellectuals, particularly Julius Nyereres' concept of self-reliance and Samin Amin's strategy of de-linking'. Nyereres, ex-president of Tanzania, tried to integrate traditional and intellectual ideas proposing modernisation that is based on human development values, including equality and freedom (Nabudeve and Simon, 2019). This modernisation (especially of rural areas) had to be self-reliant on the domestic resources.

On the other hand, Amin an Egyptian/Arab thinker, criticised innovation-led economic growth as a strategy that promotes the interests of dominant economic powers in the centre of global capitalism and at the same time contributes to underdevelopment of countries in the periphery. According to him:

> Delinking has nothing to do with exclusion or autarchic withdrawal. It is a matter of subjecting the mutual relations between the various nations and regions of the whole world of the planet to the varying imperatives of their own internal development and not the reverse.
>
> (Amin, 1990: xii)

Delinking is therefore a strategy for change, moving away from capitalism and neo-liberalism to alternative forms of development centred at people and their relations in society.

Post Development

Another reaction to the mainstream unjust innovation-led development projects of liberalism and structuralism is that of post development.

This approach, represented by authors such as Sachs (1992, 2010) and Escobar (1995) considers the modern project of innovation and development to be a lost cause and by definition unjust in both resources and relational terms. In the view of these authors, historically speaking, development was designed to cover the damage being done to developing nations through colonialism. Sachs' publication of the *Development Dictionary* in 1992 initiated this critique of the mainstream development. He also argued that 'The idea of development stands like a ruin in the intellectual landscape' (Sachs, 2010: xv) and called for dismantling the mental structure of this idea. Escobar, in his preface to the 2012 edition of his *Encountering Development*, describes post development as follows:

> Generally speaking, 'post development' arose from a poststructuralist and postcolonial critique, that is an analysis of development as a set of discourses and practices that had profound impact on how Asia, Africa and Latin America came to be seen as 'underdevelopment' and treated as such. In this context, post development was meant to designate at least three interrelated things: first, the need to decentre development … Second … post development suggested that it was indeed possible to think about the end of development … Third, post development emphasised the importance of transforming the 'political economy of truth' that is development's order of expert knowledge and power.

In some respects, the post development approach is in line with the postcolonial critique of development that rejects universality of western ideas of modernity. However, in defence of the mainstream development project, some authors point out that post development ignores the achievements of modernity in terms of freedom and justice while romantises traditional, non-western forms of public authority (Thomas, 2021). Another line of criticism is that post development does not offer clear alternatives to planned and unplanned processes of innovative and developmental change.

Alternative Development

Like post development theorists, proponents of alternative development criticise the failures of mainstream approaches to economic and social change through powerful top-down interventions. However, unlike post development theorists, proponents of alternative development don't simply reject these mainstream approaches but also propose radical new ideas for social change towards justice in development and innovation. Thomas (2021) has identified and analysed four such ideas: *political engagement*; *agency for social transformation*; *cultural diversity*; and *new theory of social change*.

First, *political engagement* is proposed as an alternative to mainstream development that is based on expertise and specialised knowledge. This engagement should promote progressive change and solidarity through non-state forces and organisations which challenge the dominant order (Ferguson, 1990). In their recent book *From Anger to Action*, Jackson and Lamb (2021) reflect on the journey to change and argue that 'So much change has come about only because citizens have imagined, acted and organised, pushing politicians to take 'new' issues seriously and creating the inspiring visions that help people to see how a better world would look' (Jackson and Lamb, 2021: 7). Indeed, other theorists and even innovation-led development practitioners also appreciate the role of civil society and activism in social change. For example, in his recent book, former CEO of Oxfam GB, Sriskandarajan (2024: 296) insists that '… people and movements are tackling the world's problems, raising awareness of hidden issues and the urgency of change … Real power lies in realising our collective identity'. As Thomas (2021) also argues, alternative and post development theorists such as Escobar have been engaging directly with activists in their native regions, e.g., Colombia.

Second, *agency* for social transformation means that people don't wait for the state but solve their own problems through local interactions and networks. This way of thinking goes back to Schumacher's argument that 'The really helpful things will not be done from the centre; they cannot be done by big organisations; but they be done by the people themselves …' (Schumacher, 1973: 205). Contemporary theorists of innovation and development reconstruct Schumacher's 'Small is Beautiful' argument by advancing the idea of inclusive innovation. They insist that '… while innovation has great potential to address a number of grand challenges (e.g. alleviating disease burden and malnutrition, eliminating poverty, delivering good health, security and sustainability) to do so successfully it must be inclusive of the needs and the interests of the poor' (Papaioannou, 2018: 2). Most of inclusive innovation is localised or community based, involving participation of people who become agents of their own development.

Third, *cultural diversity* is reflected in alternative organising concepts of society away from Westernised notions and ways of life. According to Thomas (2021: 72), 'If people and communities are empowered to develop themselves, it follows that they will do so in distinctively different ways which will be affected by a whole variety of variables: 'pluriverse' '. Cultural diversity is against uniformity and promotes different visions of living well in the planet.

Fourth, as Thomas (2021) observes, there is an emerging *theory of social change* that recognises the plurality of versions of the good society and the fact that a lot of these versions are non-Western ones. The same is the case for the plurality of knowledges at micro and macro levels. This emerging theory is in line with the project of decolonisation in the 21st century. It shares the same objective of moving away its historical ties to colonial legacies, endorsing both material and discursive decolonising efforts. These efforts point towards recognising alternative historical and contemporary views of development coming from the global South and destabilise the ethnocentric foundations of development.

All four ideas of alternative innovation and development appear to emphasise non-ideal and above all relational claims of justice from the bottom up. In this sense, they are in line with similar theoretical developments in innovation. Both innovation and development seem to endorse the move from ideal principles to non-ideal principles and from focus on material resources to focus on social relations.

3.6 Concluding Remarks

In this chapter, I argued that development, like innovation, is not a straightforward concept. Its meaning is not necessarily about good or just change. However, development is interrelated to justice and therefore the same questions of non-ideal justice apply. Development, of course, has been heavily contested in terms of both theory and practice. Two key approaches to development have been distinguished. The first is 'little d' development that conceives change as an unplanned process of the capitalist market. The second is 'big D' development that conceives change as a planned process of the state. Both approaches are underpinned by specific notions of justice which characterised the post-World War II project of development. The latter focused predominantly on innovation-driven economic growth. Clearly, this project has failed to deliver substantial reduction of poverty and relational inequality let alone increase of prosperity. Therefore, a third approach to development emerged as a critique of traditional planned and unplanned change. This is the so-called approach to post development. Post development is in line with non-ideal and relational justice in innovation because it promotes public action for achieving relational and egalitarian goals.

4 The Case of Emerging Technologies

Emerging technologies ought to be a concern for non-ideal justice in both innovation and development. This is not only because of their well-documented impact on individual and collective decisions, but also because of the fact such impact is predominantly relational. Noble (2018: 171) presents her research findings on unequal representation of black women and other minorities through online search engines such as Google, concluding that, in the 21st century,

> we have more data and technology than ever in our daily lives and more social, political, and economic inequality and injustice to go with it.

To address these phenomena, a non-ideal justice in innovation and development needs to investigate systematically and in detail claims of relational oppression, domination, and exploitation. Understanding these claims in both global North and global South contexts presupposes that we systematically draw on theories of justice and innovation as well as on theories of justice and development. Noble argues that search engines oppress and discriminate on the grounds of value-laden algorithms. Therefore, internet platforms, interfaces and software are not innocent technical innovations which simply contribute development of people and countries. Instead, they are shaped by economic imperatives, power and values of dominant people and countries (mainly in the global North) to become themselves sources of domination and oppression. Through them, few powerful people in the global North can control computer programs and software, offering little choice and freedom to publics in the global South.

DOI: 10.4324/9781003652083-5

This chapter argues that innovators, regulators, and publics who respectively generate, regulate, and use emerging technologies are obliged to enable (and not block) the creation of an innovative society of equals in non-ideal terms. As Freeman et al (1971) used to insist, these actors are essential for the responsible use of science and technology. Responsibility implies reduction of inequality as a social and economic implication of science-driven innovation. Thus, to paraphrase Freeman et al (Freeman et al, 1971), technological innovation and development cannot be divorced from their social implications and applications, and innovators regulators and users cannot escape their individual and social responsibilities. Technologies such as the Internet of Things (IoT: interconnection of computer devices and sensors through the Internet allowing communication and exchange of data between them) and artificial intelligence (AI: computers' evolving capacity to take on tasks which require some form of intelligence) and machine learning (ML: computers' evolving capacity to recognise patterns in data and make predictions) ought to be designed in such way that address challenges in our digital world from the perspective of equity, recognition and participation. The application of these bottom-up principles in innovation and development processes is crucial for ensuring just outcomes from a relational perspective. This, however, implies that the distributive perspective is also presupposed. If it is for everyone to be enabled to relate equally to one another, then it is for everyone to be enabled to meet their resource needs. Without satisfying the latter condition, the former cannot be achieved.

The chapter is divided into three sections. Section 4.1 is focused on non-ideal obligations of emerging technologies. Section 4.2 outlines some challenges in digital world. Section 4.3 considers implications for global development. Section 4.4 discusses the Covid-19 pandemic as a turning point for the acceleration of innovative technologies, and the potential relational injustices they create.

4.1 Non-Ideal Obligations of Emerging Technologies

In the so-called fourth industrial revolution, there is consensus for the need to steer accelerating technological shifts at different scales and towards more inclusive outcomes. Especially in the developing world, this need is unquestionable. In 2016, approximately 1.2 billion people lacked access to electricity (IEA, 2016). Since then, the situation has worsen given the energy crisis in 2022 that followed the Russia's invasion of Ukraine. Currently, more than 4 million people die from indoor air pollution due to lack of clean energy and 800,000 children die each year from preventable diseases. What is even more worrying, is that the rate of poverty reduction has halved since 2013 (World Bank, 2018) and extreme poverty is increasing in certain areas such as in Sub-Saharan Africa. This trend has become worse in the aftermath of the Covid-19 pandemic. As projections by Hoy and Sumner (2020) indicate, countries will need to achieve historically unprecedented growth levels to reduce poverty and achieve Sustainable Development Goals (SDGs) by 2030. As such, the SDGs seem to reflect the consensus for both the need of relational justice in innovation and the need of economic growth. In this sense, they redefine the mission of science, technology, and innovation as the further reduction of poverty and the elimination of extreme deprivation.

Clearly then, if relational injustice is (and ought to be) a foundational concept in innovation and development, it is crucial to investigate the non-ideal obligations of emerging technologies which impact on development. By non-ideal obligations, I mean a set of obligations emanating from the bottom-up principles of equity, recognition, and participation. These are obligations towards innovators, regulators, and public users of emerging technologies. They range from non-discrimination against people of colour, low income, gender, etc., to recognition of their freedom and equality as well as to importance of their participation in the shaping of such technologies. Cleary, emerging innovative technologies are already diffusing in key development areas such as education, healthcare, agriculture, gig economy platforms, and humanitarian assistance. For example, in healthcare, technologies such as the IoT are creating value by allowing personalisation of treatments and rapid data collection; AI and ML are providing more accurate diagnosis of some diseases than doctors. In agriculture, AI technologies are enabling the monitoring of crops and automating harvesting and optimising timing. Also, facial recognition technologies, AI-driven gig economy applications, click-work developments in labour markets are proliferating. In humanitarian assistance, digital technologies have become indispensable for operations in conflict and disaster zones. According to Madianou (2019: 2):

> Most UN agencies now have innovation labs and data departments. Refugee registration by default involve biometric data which are outsourced to private vendors, part of multimillion, rapidly

> expanding biometric industry. Large datasets are being used for needs assessment and the coordination of aid while artificial intelligence (AI) is being explored to track displaced people and predict population flows and future crises.

All these examples indicate that emerging technologies have been already integrated in peoples' everyday lives, and they don't even notice, or they consider them as given.

According to Rise (2018), in the 21st century, AI and ML technologies promise to make more accurate predictions of our habits, drive cars more safely than we do, take care of our health, etc. Such emerging technological innovations question the implicit assumption of hierarchical superiority of humankind. Superintelligent machines are no longer a futuristic scenario. They are a fact that has been already experienced in the global North and diffusing rapidly in the global South. In Rise's view, new generations might even grow up with intelligent machines and therefore might be attached to them in such ways that would prevent them from switching-off. He uses three examples to illustrate his argument:

> Already in 2007, a US Colonel called off a robotic land-sweeping exercise because he considered the operation inhumane after a robot kept crawling along losing legs one at time … A humanoid robot named Sophia with capabilities to participate in interviews, developed by Hanson Robotics, became a Saudi citizen in October 2017. Later Sophia was named UNDP's first-ever innovation champion. … Jeff Bezos recently adopted a dog called SpotMini, a versatile robotic pet capable of opening doors, picking himself up and even loading the dishwasher.

Apart from deeper and rather long-term philosophical questions of consciousness and morality of superintelligence that Rise (2018) raises, there are also short-term questions of justice which concern the kind of world and the form of development these innovations shape. If one takes development to be a planned process (i.e. big D development) then one might be possible to imagine superintelligent machines dealing with knowledge gaps in every aspect of policymaking and implementation. From structuralist, dependency, and interventionist perspectives, superintelligent machines might be useful policy tools as long as they can be politically controlled. By contrast, if one takes development to be an unplanned process (i.e. little d development) then one might be possible to imagine the unintended consequences of superintelligent machines creating institutions such as those Hayek (1960) defined as a spontaneous orders, i.e., self-organising, complex systems that arise endogenously without the involvement of deliberate human design (Hayek, 1973; Papaioannou, 2012). From liberal, neo-liberal and modernisation perspectives, policy might enable such spontaneity, avoiding political intervention into the consequences of superintelligent machines.

Emerging technologies often become part of what Jimenez et al (2025: 2) call 'innovation speak' that instead of promoting inclusion and equity, it aligns with the interests of national elites and aspirations of privileged groups. Critical innovation studies (Walsh, 2021; Fougere and Harding, 2012; Thomas et al, 2017) have also stressed the depoliticised and imperialistic nature of dominant 'innovation speak' revealing its one-dimensional focus on technological and commercial aspects, and its tendency towards homogenisation and hegemonisation. The dominant innovation speak also abstracts from potential harmful consequences of emerging technologies. To use the words of Sveiby et al (2012: 6) '… those who innovate and support innovation do not necessarily see the need to take responsibility for or even consider consequences'. Phenomena of harmful biases and discrimination of some emerging technologies have already taken place not only in global South but also in global North.

Take for instance, women and gender relations. There are already documented algorithm biases against women, e.g., computers sending management level job alerts to more men than women. Eubanks (2018) shows how data mining, policy algorithms and predictive risk models impact unfairly on poor communities. In her view:

> migrants, unpopular religious groups, sexual minorities, the poor and other oppressed and exploited populations bear much higher burden of monitoring and tracking than advantaged groups.

By arguing so Eubanks identifies a fundamental relational injustice in innovation that exacerbates the already unequal treatment of poor and working class communities. Her work along with the work of other scholars, including Masiero (2016) and O'Neill (2016), show that 'dataveilance' (Taylor, 2017) disadvantages the poor. Nationally, dataveillance is used to assure that people are not abusing welfare funds and undocumented immigrants are tracked by digital systems (Taylor, 2017: 2). In practice, these technologies are used to enforce exclusion within cities or countries and create conditions for making disadvantaged individuals and their communities feel unwelcome.

Globally, there is an increasing number of data-driven discrimination cases. According to Taylor (2017) one of them is the following:

> India's biometric population database, known as Aadhar. The database is the World's largest with over a billion records and was launched in 2009 with the stated aim of combating welfare fraud … However, the design of technologies … in fact ensures that the poorest are the worst served by Aadhar. The system's design does not acknowledge the materiality of poverty, being unable to 'authenticate those who work with stone, cement, limestone and those over the age of 60'.

Aadhar has been developed without any involvement of the poor and the marginalised. Instead, it has been designed by powerful elites to maintain high level of relational inequality in society. Aadhar is now mandatory for anyone who wants to access the Indian welfare system. However, as Arun (2020: 598) observes, '… it has been criticised for excluding people from this welfare system owing to the many ways in which it malfunctions. Researchers have found that up to twenty-seven deaths from 2015 have been directly linked to Aadhar. The database has also been breached several times, and news reports say that almost a billion records with personally identifiable information have been compromised'.

Similarly to Taylor and Arun, as has been already mentioned at opening of this chapter, Noble (2018) provides strong evidence for the fact that search engines such as Google often reinforce racially and gendered attitudes against people of colour and sexual minorities. She demonstrates how algorithms, as value-ladden propositions, implicate global racial power relations. Issues of equity, recognition and participation have to be addressed in the innovative processes of designing digital platforms and software.

The fact is that the already fast diffusion of benefits of innovative technologies to global North and global South populations are currently very unequal, leaving too many individuals and their societies behind. On the one hand, as we have seen, the diffusion of risks overwhelmingly affects individuals and social groups who find themselves marginalised and excluded. On the other hand, AI/ML has been evidently used by political regimes to suppress, e.g., the mass surveillance of China's Uyghur minority, the censoring of people's free expression in Russia, etc. As Jones (2023: 8) points out:

> Many AI tools abuse human rights as a collateral consequence of their operation. AI risks embedding and exaggerating bias and discrimination invading privacy, reducing personal autonomy, and making society more, rather than less, unequal. For example, AI sentencing tools may discriminate against minorities, potentially turning back decades of progress towards equality. AI in healthcare may harm human health if algorithms are incorrect or biased, while AI in welfare-provision or migration may make unfair decisions to eligibility.

AI also poses threats to democracies due to manipulation of politics and electorates through spreading fake information, whether images, news videos, etc.

Drawing on all these examples of risks arising from emerging technologies, one can argue that no justice demands of equity, recognition and participation seem to be met through the current governance of such innovative technologies. In fact, innovative technologies currently appear to reflect relations of inequality in the process of innovation generation and diffusion, prioritising some needs (of high-income individuals and societies) and marginalising others (of low-income individuals and societies). The latter needs are basic needs but often fail to be communicated into innovation process through participation. In a recent paper, Jones (2023: 7) argues that

> properly managed, AI can enable delivery of the UN's Sustainable Development Goals (SDGs) by the 2030 deadline, boost the implementation of social and cultural rights worldwide, and support improvements in many areas of life.

However, proper management of AI and other emerging technologies presupposes a clear set of justice obligations embedded in innovation process.

4.2 The Challenges in Digital World

Certainly, in an increasingly digital world, big data analytics, AI/ML and the IoT challenge traditional obligations of justice and equality, threatening the essence of human rights, i.e., inviolability of human life (Risse, 2018). Human rights include individual rights to privacy but also rights to autonomy, freedom of thought, freedom of expression, freedom of association, and freedom of conscience and religion. Emerging AI technologies can potentially violate these obligations through applications which are not based on moral and legal judgements. Take for example big data; it can potentially undermine the right to security and the right privacy. Take another example of emotion recognition; it can potentially undermine the right to autonomy.

Given that individuals are the producers and the users of data through interconnected devices which can monitor their everyday lives and health, the question of who owns (and who ought to own) these data become fundamental. Within capitalism, the type of ownership promoted is private ownership of big data and related benefits. This is mainly justified in broad libertarian terms through the notion of inviolable individual rights to private property. As has been already pointed out in Chapter 1, ideal theorists such as Nozick and his followers defended absolute individual right to private property whereas liberal egalitarian theorists such as Rawls and his followers introduce principles of justice which allow redistribution of privately owned data and related benefits to the least well-off of society. By contrast, relational and non-ideal theories of justice are more interested in the impact of privately owned data and related benefits on how people relate to one another (in equal or unequal terms). Ownership is a predominantly social relationship that ought to be governed by equity, recognition, and participation. Otherwise, such relationship is unjust and impacts negatively on a possible society of equals.

There have been already several court cases, challenging the application of AI/ML technologies from a human rights perspective. Jones (2023) outlines some of these cases. They include the 2022 case of

> the UK NGO Big Brother Watch [that] issued a legal complaint to the British information commissioner in respect of alleged use of facial recognition technology by Facewatch and the supermarket chain Southern Co-op to scan, maintain and assess profiles of all supermarket visitors'.
>
> (Jones, 2023: 47)

Also, the 2020 case of

> the Hague district court that ordered the Dutch government to cease its use of SyRI, an automated programme that reviewed the

> personal data of social security claimants to predict how likely people were to commit benefit or tax fraud … The court found that the legislation regulating SyRI did not comply with the right to respect for private life in Article 8 ECHR.

In these cases, human rights law demanded governments and companies to cease breaching their obligations and responsibilities. However, in other cases, it has not been clear who bears moral and legal responsibility (or who is obliged) for the operation of AI/ML systems. Is the developer(s) (the innovators) of an AI/ML system who has to answer questions of human rights and justice or is the deployer (the publics) of the system who uses it in a away for which it was not intended and hence they need to be held to account from a moral perspective (Jones, 2023) or is the governor(s) (the regulators) of an AI/ML system who has a duty to de-risk the system or is the AI/ML system itself morally responsible for the outcomes it generate?

Certainly, these questions are not easy to address especially with regards moral responsibility. What conditions one ascribes to moral responsibility depends on one's moral principles. In a recent article, Constantinescu et al (2022) try to provide answers by drawing on Aristotelian ethics but recognising at the same time the diversity of approaches to moral responsibility. According to them:

> contemporary philosophical discussions seem to revolve around two main conditions to ascribe moral responsibility: the freedom and the epistemic conditions. These conditions are either implicitly or explicitly, acknowledged to be rooted in Aristotle's work on criteria to ascribe moral blame or praise the agent. First, the freedom or control (of action) condition concerns the possibility of moral responsibility in lack of free will, discussing whether moral responsibility is compatible or not with (causal) determinism … Second, the epistemic or knowledge condition refers to the possibility of moral responsibility when the agent lacks either relevant information about circumstances of their action or advanced moral understanding of the implications of their actions.
>
> (Constantinescu et al, 2022: 4)

Both conditions imply that an agent (whether innovator, regulator, public or a technology) can be ascribed moral responsibility if and only if:

a an agent is knowledgeable of the facts pertaining their actions (epistemic condition); and
b they chose their actions without being coerced or constrained by others (freedom condition).

For the outcomes of emerging technologies such as AI and ML, the technologies themselves cannot be held morally responsible simply because neither the epistemic nor the freedom condition is in place. Machines can only be knowledgeable of the facts they are trained with, and they are constrained by the rules of innovators, regulators and publics.

If what I argue is correct, then moral responsibility for the outcomes of emerging technologies can only be ascribed to innovators, regulators, and publics. Depending on how knowledgeable and free each of these actors is to direct emerging technologies towards just outcomes, each bears moral responsibility for their actions.

Big data as such can be regarded as a means of production in digital world. AI and ML technologies require thousands of words, images, audio, numbers, and other data in order for them to provide answer to specific questions or to make a prediction. ML technologies can find patterns in existing big data and be trained to make predictions for unseen data. In this sense, such technologies enable AI that is mainly concerned with the creation of intelligent systems through algorithms. The latter simply learn to imitate models build to provide answers on things like credit-scoring of borrowers, behaviour patterns of consumers, etc. For example, a credit scoring algorithm might be trained to learn patterns in the repayment history of past borrowers to determine or predict the repayment behaviour of future borrowers. One or another way, ownership of big data that enables such technologies determines whether they can be used for promoting a society of equals or instead promoting a society in which inequality, exploitation and oppression dominate relations between people. As Rise (2018: 12) points out

> Unequal ownership of data will have detrimental consequences for many people in society … if the power of companies such as Alphabet, Apple, Facebook or Tesla is not harnessed for the public good, we might eventually find ourselves in a world dominated by companies.

In the same line of argument, theorists of data justice such as Heeks and Renken (2018) point out the importance of the right of people to decide, choose and use data. Bearing in mind that innovators, regulators, and publics are both producers and users of data, everyone ought to have access to the data and related services. Otherwise, quality of life might be compromised.

Of course, unjust relations of domination and oppression are no longer future scenarios. Well-known data scandals such as those of Cambridge-Analytica in the UK and Facebook in the US (2018) reveal the need for governance and regulatory frameworks which enforce non-ideal obligations of equity, recognition, and participation for emerging technologies. The technologies themselves are unable to make judgements about fairness. One issue here is processing and considering what Hume called circumstances of justice. This refers to the background circumstances of human action which enable plausible decisions about whether such action is just or unjust. Circumstances encompass personal, cultural, institutional, and other aspects of human action. In order for a moral and/or legal judgement to be made, there is a need for critical engagement with and dialogue about circumstances of justice. Emerging AI and ML technologies are not able to meet the requirements of delivering plausible moral and legal judgements, especially in cases where the circumstances of justice are complex. This implies their non-ideal obligations of equity, recognition and participation require humans to implement them in specific applications. Certainly, these obligations derive from the very nature of innovation that is predominantly co-operative and is based on recognition of equal respect. The advantage of principles of justice in innovation is that they can address not only issues of fair ownership, use, handling and access of data (Heeks and Renken, 2018) but also issues of equal relations, respect and participation. This implies that non-ideal principles of justice in innovation can guide change in the very process of generation of new technologies and not just their ownership. In some respects, these principles address the old Marxist distinction between (technological) forces and (social) relations of production that tended to ignore there exist structural inequalities even within conditions of equal ownership of new technologies (Feenberg, 1991).

Non-ideal principles of relational justice in innovation and development do not justify governments and/or companies to use online data surveillance to identify potential opponents or customers. In addition, they don't allow the undemocratic and unequal development of algorithms which reinforce oppressive social relations and promote racial profiling of people. As Noble (2018: 2) demonstrates

> some of the very people who are developing search algorithms and architecture are willing to promote sexist and racist attitudes openly at work and beyond that these same employees are developing 'neutral' or 'objective' decision-making tools. Human beings are developing the digital platforms we use.

Governance and regulatory frameworks which derive from non-ideal principles of relational justice in innovation focus on technologies themselves. This means, they do not stop innovation but instead aim to prevent big data applications in certain sectors from exacerbating relational and structural inequalities at national and global levels. This has further impact on governance and regulation of AI that is based on algorithms. As Dignum (2022) notes, an algorithm is nothing more than a recipe that includes a set of rules towards achieving a certain result, say baking an apple pie.

> However, by itself, the recipe has never turned into an apple pie; and the end result of your pie has much to do with your baking skills and your choice of ingredients, as with the choice for a specific recipe. The same applies to algorithms: for a large part of the behaviour and results of the system depends on its input data, on the choices made by those that developed, trained and selected the algorithm.
>
> (Dignum, 2022: 4)

Dignum concludes that in the same way we have choices about what apples to use in a pie, in AI we also have choices to use data that respects and ensures fairness, privacy, etc. From this it follows that principles of equity, recognition and participation can be used in AI as well as in other emerging technologies provided political choices can be made towards this direction. Training an AI system to avoid bias and discrimination, ensuring justice in innovation, is possible. Also, measuring and correcting the performance of an AI system against normative benchmarks can be achieved.

One approach might be to make the principles of justice in innovation an internal algorithm design criterion. This is a specific ethical approach to AL and ML technologies. It resonates with Carter's suggestion about a moral dimension of AI-assisted decision-making. According to him '... like software of nearly any kind, AI algorithms are the product of many hands and many engineers working in many venues over many years' (Carter, 2020: 302). For these engineers, making ethics an internal design criterion '... can be as exciting as maximising any other design feature, especially if value is attributed to it' (Carter, 2020).

An additional approach might be, according to Carter (2020), to focus on the process of algorithm design and introduce dual or multiple checks by experts with equal ethics training. It might be suggested that such training must cover the principles of relational egalitarian justice in innovation. Establishing a design control process according to principles of relational egalitarian justice might reduce the likelihood of moral errors with advanced AI applications and prevent innovators from enabling moral catastrophes.

In any case, independently of whether making principles of justice in innovation an internal algorithm design criterion or establishing a design control process is the best possible approach to dealing with moral obligations of relational egalitarian justice in innovation, one should also ask the question of the role of politics and government in regulating emerging technologies. According to Jones (2023: 34):

> Governments are increasingly considering cross-sectoral regulation of AI on the basis that statutory obligations would help create a level of playing field for safe and ethical AI and bolster consumer trust, while mitigating the risk that pre-AI regulation applies to AI in haphazard fashion. The EU is furthest along in this process with its draft AI Act that would ban the highest-risk forms of AI and subject other 'high-risk' AI to conformity assessments. In the US, Congress is considering a draft Algorithmic Accountability Act. The British government, having considered the case of cross-cutting AI regulation has recently announced plans for non-statutory, context specific approach that aims to be pro-innovation and to focus primarily on high-risk concerns.

The main debate, as implied above, is whether general regulation of AI and ML technologies will risk stopping innovation and development. A recent report presented by Sir Patrick Vallance, the UK Government Chief Scientific Adviser, as part of the *Pro-Innovation Regulation of Technologies Review*, indeed takes the view that '... the government should avoid regulating emerging digital technologies too early to avoid the risk of stifling innovation' (HM Government, 2023: 13). The review recommends that government regulators should continue to engage with industry on issues such as safety, risks and benefits of innovation. However, it might be argued that unless other public actors, including bottom-up activist groups and social movements, are enabled to participate in this engagement process, non-ideal principles of justice in innovation would be ignored for the sake of narrow industrial interests which mainly anticipate increase of profits, due to AI and ML technological expectations. Bottom-up engagement with regulators can lead to developing justified socio-technological processes to ensure AI and other emerging technologies deliver just outcomes.

4.3 Implications for Development

It is clear that development policy and practice ought to understand the point of equality in emerging technologies such as AI/ML systems as being primarily relational and not predominantly distributional. This implies that investigating claims and/or identifying relational inequalities, because of algorithmic (intended or unintended) mistakes which affect disproportionally minorities and marginalised groups (e.g. failure of commercial face-detection systems to notice dark-skinned faces) or because of data bias towards the poor and vulnerable members of society (e.g. failure of algorithms to identify children at risk for abuse in wealthy families and instead overwhelmingly focusing on poor families which receive public assistance) is the first key task of development policymakers. The causes of relational inequality in innovation are multi-dimensional and hence complex. Understanding this complexity is crucial for rectifying relational inequalities in innovation, and ensuring just and inclusive development.

Development policymakers also need to ensure that the actual process of rectification of relational injustices in innovation involves non-ideal solutions for 'trial and error'. Such solutions should be able to pass the feasibility test so that they can settle claims of relational injustice in the best possible way. Take for example a claim of failure of commercial face-detection of dark-skinned faces. To address it, policymakers might try different non-ideal solutions, e.g., re-development and/or retraining algorithms so that they can treat everyone as equal (Binns, 2018). AI/ML systems rely on training data which have been collected in advance. Such collection of data should observe principles of equity and recognition and participation. If any of the proposed solutions in the above example prevents commercial face-detection systems from discriminating against dark-skinned faces, then it can be potentially regarded as successful and thereby settle the claim of relational injustice. Take as another example a claim of failure of algorithms to decentre whiteness and racial oppression in academia. To address this claim of coloniality, public policy might try different solutions, e.g., regulating and/or standardising against algorithmic decision-making systems which rely on Eurocentric epistemologies; retraining algorithms to eliminate digital elements of decolonisation and racialisation (Dignum, 2022). If any of these solutions works in the sense of settling claims of coloniality, then policy can conclude that some level of equalisation of relations has been achieved.

Another task for development policy and practice is to ensure resources are equally distributed within and between countries so that the demands of relational egalitarian justice in innovation and development are met. For example, in Africa, relational injustices in innovation are driven by distributive injustices such as the digital divide. As Gill and Germann (2022: 299) point out

> In 2030, of the global population of 8.55 billion, 39% or 3.31 billion would be children under 15 years of age. Almost one third of them would live in Africa. These young people, many of whom may well be digital natives, could be tremendous asset given the right educational and economic opportunity. However, if existing inequities continue to fest, exacerbated by a lack of access and agency driven by persistent 'digital divide' the incredible opportunity of a skilled and engaged 'youth bulge' would be missed, resulting in a lost generation.

Africa is a place where AI/ML technologies are very unequally developed and used in businesses in agriculture, in healthcare and education. Dealing with insufficient digital literacy and unequal computing skills, and lack of infrastructure will have positive impact on mitigating relational injustices. However, as Coeckelbergh (2022: vii) stress '… Africa is not a country; it is a continent (in fact the second largest on earth) and a very diverse one'. This fact indicates the level of complexity that public policy needs to deal with in providing the resources for reducing distributive and relational injustices through AI/ML technologies.

Currently, young people in Nigeria, Mauritius, Ghana, Kenya and South Africa seem to have higher level of digital literacy and skills compared to the rest of sub-Saharan Africa (Choi et al, 2020). AI and ML giants such as Facebook and Microsoft rely on such skills to expand in Africa. In 2020, Facebook announced a multimillion-dollar cable to interconnect 23 countries in Africa. Microsoft in 2017 invested in bringing Internet connectivity in rural areas of Ghana, Nigeria, Kenya, South Africa, Zambia, Rwada, Tanzania, and Democratic Republic of Congo. In parallel, a number of Chinese companies provide digital and telecom services to African countries (Okolo et al, 2023) These investments are driven by expectations about further development of digital technologies and related skills in Africa.

Although, as Kaplinsky (2021) points out, digital technological and development expectations in Africa and other developing nations are high, they are also accompanied by concerns of social responsibility and environmental sustainability. For example, recent research indicates that increasingly many AI/ML models such as GPT-5 (perhaps also including models of artificial moral advisors) are trained and deployed on energy- and water-hungry servers in data centres with enormous carbon footprint. According to Li et al (2023: 2) the combined on-site and off-site

> global water withdrawal of Google, Microsoft and Meta reached an estimate of 2.2 billion cube waters in 2022, equivalent to the total annual water withdrawal (including municipal, industrial, and agricultural usage) of two Denmark … Simultaneously, out of the total water withdrawal, approximately 0.18 billion cubic metters (including 0.13 billion cubic meters in the US) was 'lost' to evaporation and hence considered 'consumption' which was even more than the total water withdrawal in Liberia (a country of about 5 million people in West Africa).

In Africa, development policy and practice need to deal with crucial trade-offs between technological development and sustainability and social inclusion.

The bottom line of just AI/ML systems for development is that they can enable innovators, regulators, and publics to participate as equals in social co-operation. This notion of relational egalitarian justice allows for some limited distributive inequality to be tolerated only so long as the requirements of relational egalitarian justice can be met. However, if these requirements cannot be met due to trade-offs between technological development and sustainability, then distributive inequality is no longer justified and need to be reduced.

4.4 The Covid-19 Turning Point

In 2020, the global outbreak of Covid-19 has exacerbated innovation injustice phenomena such a dataveilance. As countries, including China, Singapore, South Korea, Hong Kong, and others, raced to contain the virus, dataveillance technologies were deployed to monitor individuals' health and movements. A proliferation of government-mandated apps, enabling collection of private information such as location of individuals, names, and national ID numbers, has raised serious concerns about violation of human rights and fears of normalising future surveillance.

These examples of national and global uses of innovation reveal two things:

1 Moral and political distinctions between deserving and undeserving poor are embedded in certain technologies leading to unjust outcomes. These technologies are, in fact, signalling out the poor and disadvantaged for insulting levels of scrutiny (Li et al, 2023), eventually excluding them from processes of social reproduction and stigmatising them. Eubanks (2018) and Noble (2018) demonstrate empirically the devastating consequences of application of unjust technologies on the lives of poor people in the US.
2 Authoritarian states deploy emerging detaveilance technologies, violating individual rights to privacy and freedom for the sake of responding to health or other emergencies. This also tends to disproportionately affect the already disadvantaged given that communicable disease outbreaks thrive in poor and densely populated areas of the developed and developing world. People in those areas are often stigmatised and/or disadvantaged as potentially infectious and virus spreaders.

As early as in 2016, Practical Action called to public action for addressing innovation and development injustice, moving beyond nation state borders, and demanding an urgent paradigm shift in top-down approach to innovation, technology, and international development (Practical Action, 2016). According to Practical Action

(Practical Action, 2016) we must improve access to technologies so that we can ensure people meet their essential needs and develop governance mechanisms that can effectively curb the use of technologies which damage the environment.

It might be maintained that such a paradigm shift in the global approach to innovation and development presupposes that public action succeeds to legitimise technologies which comply (even partially) with non-ideal principles of equity, recognition, and participation. Some theorists, including Heeks and Renken (2018) and Taylor (2017), attempt to integrate different aspects of justice in innovation, e.g., data justice into the overarching framework of Sen's capability approach, emphasising the importance of freedoms that people value with regard new technologies. Indeed, this approach embeds non-ideal principles of equity, recognition, and participation which can be operationalised in different contexts. In this sense, in different contexts, governance and regulation ought to require fairer share of benefits and risks of innovation in order to increase capabilities and establish a society of equals. This is crucial for changing the direction of innovation systems towards delivering technologies for just social, economic and environmental outcomes. Failure to do so could exacerbate technological anxiety in the era of fourth technological revolution.

In his last book *Innovation and Its Enemies: Why People Resist New Technologies*, technology enthusiast Calestous Juma (2016: 5) tries to explain why people turn against technological innovation when it is clear that some emerging technologies can enable people to achieve progress and higher standards of living. His explanation revolves around anxiety and controversies of emerging technologies. Juma argues that such anxiety and controversies arise from the following tension:

> the need to innovate and the pressure to maintain continuity, social order and stability … The tension between novelty and stability arising from transformational innovation is a leading source of public controversies and policy challenges.

It might be suggested that maintenance of continuity, social order and stability depends on whether transformational innovation is in fact socially just. The proliferation of new digital technologies requires politics and public policy to engage in foresight exercises and advanced assessments of the potentially unjust and disruptive effects of innovation over decades. Indeed, as Juma (2016: 292) also recognises:

> In most cases, opposition to new technologies arises from a sense of exclusion. It is about understanding the subtle distinctions between technology as products and technology as platforms for generating new solutions that may not be priority of the sales departments of foreign firms. It is not a surprise though that the absence of inclusive strategies leads to intense debates over questions of justice … The case for inclusive innovation is even more urgent and income disparities around the world become increasingly associated with technological innovation.

Juma's argument clearly considers justice in innovation and development to be a key factor for the legitimacy and the scaling up of emerging technologies. Claims for equal participation, recognition and access to these technologies fall into this category of justice. Public activists and campaigners for justice try to make explicit that innovation is inherently political. Indeed, as Smith and Stirling (2018: 65–66) stress:

> Too often, the very real politics of innovation is masked by technocratic and exclusive approaches imposing narrow criteria of efficiency, profit and convenience. The dominant image (and practice) of innovation continues to focus upon rent-seeking, technology-based firms working with research institutes and investors, aided by a policy environment that facilitates systemic interaction between these institutions in the pursuit of economic growth. Overlooked are the ways these arrangements privilege certain values, interests and positions towards innovation in society, and carry with them a less democratic politics than might be merited by the stakes at hand.

Public activists and campaigners are fully aware of the political fact that innovations shape people's lives and impact on social institutions in profound and pervasive ways (Smith and Stirling, 2018). By responding to injustice, they try to equalise and democratise social relations and institutional structures. Structural changes are required in order for innovators, regulators, and publics to be related equally with one another vis-à-vis new technologies and processes. For this reason, the outcomes of public action and campaigning ought to be incorporated into political decisions about the direction of innovation. Such decisions need to be more engaged with and informed by counter-hegemonic movements which defend alternatives from the bottom up. Otherwise, there is a risk for emerging technologies to enable '… the continuation of power and privilege structures, the potential echoing of colonial histories and imbalanced representation in decision making' (Roche et al, 2023: 1095).

4.5 Concluding Remarks

This chapter has sought to critically reflect on the application of a non-ideal theory of relational justice in innovation and development, focusing on emerging technologies. The argument put forward is that innovators, regulators, and public users of digital technologies cannot ignore obligations towards creating an innovative society of equals. The reason being the potential of these technologies for exacerbating oppressive and exploitative relations through lack of equity, recognition, and participation in the design and application of algorithms. As the next chapter will show, politics is presupposed of any plausible process of directing innovation and development towards just outcomes. Without politics, the direction of innovation and development can only be left to the unplanned process of the free market to decide. However, such decision cannot possibly involve considerations of non-ideal relational justice and fairness. The market is not a process that by itself can deliver just outcomes. Instead, there is certain level of moral arbitrariness when it comes to consequences of the free market process. It is politics that ensures the just direction of innovation and development. But politics ought to be democratic. For this reason, it needs to take account of public action and campaigning for relational justice in emerging technologies. Traditional liberal and structuralist notions of the state are unable to provide a framework within which bottom-up principles and actions can play a role in this process of innovation directionality.

5 Directionality of Innovation and Development

The case of emerging technologies and their potential to exacerbate existing relational injustices in innovation and development demonstrates the importance of providing directionality to their rapidly evolving trajectory. To put it another way, the question of directionality of innovation and development is central in the debate about justice of emerging technologies. In Chapter 2, I touched upon the contribution of contemporary innovation theorists such as Mazzucato and Block to revisiting the relationship between politics and innovation. This chapter and the next one will be devoted to critical discussion of this relationship with focus on innovation directionality and the role of the state. Contemporary innovation theorists (Mazzucato, 2014; Perez, 2002; Fagerberg et al, 2013; Block and Keller, 2011) tend to defend a combination of Schumpeterian and Keynesian politics of innovation and development as a solution to the problem of directionality of emerging technologies towards socially just outcomes. These theorists tend to argue from (neo) structuralist and (neo) interventionist perspectives and implicitly agree that such combined politics is crucial for transformative change, accomplishing missions such as tackling climate change, reducing poverty and inequality, and dealing with pandemics. Their hope is that the Schumpeterian motor of innovation (i.e. profit) would keep entrepreneurs incentivised to take up market opportunities while the Keynesian state would support them by investing in infrastructure, redistributing risks and rewards of new technologies.

In contrast, Hayekian theorists of innovation (Worstall, 2013; Mingardi, 2015; Wennberg and Sandström, 2022) argue from neoliberal and modernisation perspectives and insist that top-down state

DOI: 10.4324/9781003652083-6

interventions in the free market, aiming at directionality, suffer from epistemological and moral problems. On the one hand, there is lack of detailed knowledge of innovation and development dynamics in the process of competition and on the other there is a moral risk of coercion of individual entrepreneurs by the state. For Hayekian theorists of innovation, politics ought to abandon the idea of directionality of innovation towards social justice altogether because it is morally questionable and creates disincentives for taking up new risky ventures in the market. Instead, politics of innovation and development ought to be restricted to promoting a spontaneous institutional environment that is conducive to freedom and entrepreneurship.

This chapter argues that, despite differences, both combined Schumpeterian- Keynesian and Hayekian theoretical camps rely on notions of morality and politics which are predominantly ideal and tend to justify distributional currencies of justice. In this sense, they seem to overlook questions of relational equality in the process of generation and diffusion of new technologies. Therefore, they fail to go far enough to mitigate unjust relations of exploitation, domination, and oppression within processes of production and diffusion of novel technologies and goods. Although such mitigation would also presuppose certain level of equal distribution of risks and rewards of innovation, this level would not be absolute and therefore it would allow for incentives of innovative entrepreneurship to be maintained. What really matters for the trajectory of innovation towards social justice is to introduce non-ideal principles (from the bottom-up and the grassroots innovation movements) and related politics which don't reproduce unequal social relations but instead try to equalise them through appropriate level of distribution of risks and rewards of innovation. The advantage of this relational approach vis-à-vis liberal Schumpeterian-Keynesian and Hayekian approaches is its pragmatism in identifying and addressing relational inequalities in innovation process. The objective is to mitigate such inequalities instead of moving us from the current unjust state of social relations in innovation to a perfectly just one.

The Schumpeterian-Keynesian and Hayekian approaches find it difficult to subscribe to this pragmatism due to their ideal principles, e.g., freedom and equality. Different interpretations of these principles inform either economic constructions such as the Hayekian notion of the spontaneous order of 'catallaxy' that delivers peaceful exchange (Hayek, 1967) or political constructions such as the Keynesian notion of the state as a fully rational structure that delivers full employment (Keynes, 1936, 1932). Even though Hayekians and Keynesians are not always consistent with their theoretical constructions[1], and hence they often contradict their idealism, the latter cannot be dismissed as inaccurate. Rather, it should be recognised that their idealism has been constantly undermined by the reality of policymaking of the post-World War II liberal state.

The chapter is divided into four sections. Section 5.1 discusses the Schumpeterian-Keynesian politics of innovation and development. Section 5.2 analyses the Hayekian critique of politics of directionality and its epistemological and moral foundations. Section 5.3 puts forward the argument that both theoretical camps focus on distributive justice in the innovation process and therefore a relational approach is needed for directing new technologies towards just outcomes. Section 5.4 concludes by providing a summary of the overall argument.

5.1 Schumpeterian-Keynesian Approach to Directionality

More than 100 years ago, Joseph Schumpeter argued that innovation is what drives capitalist development and economic growth. He defined innovation as

> The introduction of new goods … new methods of production … the opening of new markets … the conquest of new sources of supply … and the carrying out of new organisation of any industry.
>
> (Schumpeter, 1934: 66)

The central focus of Schumpeter's definition is on the heroic entrepreneur who sees the opportunities and introduces new combinations to increase market share and maximise profits. Without profits there would be no capitalist development. Schumpeter's entrepreneur creates a new system of values by forcing innovative products into the market and propelling technological progress. Therefore, the role of Schumpeterian politics is to enable the profit motor of innovation by sustaining a liberal institutional framework of private ownership and credit creation. Within this framework competitive capitalism can evolve as a dynamic system.

Like Marx, Schumpeter was convinced that capitalism can never be stationary but rather evolve in cycles of economic growth and depression. Yet for him, the direction of capitalism in general and of innovation in particular is unpredictable. In his Prologue to Part II of *Capitalism, Socialism and Democracy*, Schumpeter (2010: 53) asks:

> Can capitalism survive? No. I don't think it can. But this opinion of mine, like that of every other economist who has pronounced upon the subject, is completely uninteresting. What counts in any attempt at social prognosis is not Yes or No that sums up the facts and the arguments which lead up to it but those facts and arguments themselves.

Schumpeter's facts and arguments are about pervasive evolutionary change in the economy due to successive innovations which lead to capitalist development. He recognises that there may be tendencies in an observable pattern, e.g., capitalism's economic and social failure but predictions about the future cannot be made.

Schumpeter understands both uncertainty and 'creative destruction' as inevitabilities of capitalism which cannot be politically controlled in order for the system to deliver socially desirable outcomes. His understanding is echoed by Fuchs and Ziegler (2025) in their contribution to this special issue of *The Journal of Responsible Innovation* (TJRI). They argue that innovation/market creation and exnovation/market destruction go hand in hand.

It might be suggested that this is a substantial point of difference with Keynes who, in his 'The End of Laissez-Faire' argues for political control of capitalism that predominantly focuses on individualism and utilitarianism. In his account, neither individualism nor utilitarianism in the economic sphere would deliver benefits to all. Keynes rejects that laissez-faire capitalism is a harmonious evolutionary process that requires non-interference by the state. Instead, he believes that the state is a fully rational structure. In this sense, the role of government is to mitigate egoism, promoting the public good. Individuals in capitalism are focused on money-making and take economic decisions on the basis of 'animal spirits'. According to Keynes (2013: 291):

> The most important thing for government is not to do things which individuals are doing already, and to do them a little better or a little worse; but to do those things which at present are not done at all.

Keynes is preoccupied with the rational organisation of society and capitalism in order to direct economic activity towards satisfactory ways of life for all. This presupposes the end of laissez-faire policies and the start of a political economy that requires government to interfere with the competitive process of the market. In his *General Theory*, Keynes becomes more specific about this political economy that aims to mitigate rather unfair consequences of capitalism such as involuntary unemployment (Keynes, 1936).

Although neither Schumpeter nor Keynes wrote explicitly on the direction of innovation, contemporary theorists (Jacobs and Mazzucato, 2016; Mazzucato, 2014; Fagerberg et al, 2013; Block and Keller, 2011) tend to combine the politics of these thinkers in order to address the question of transformative change towards socially just and desirable outcomes. As Schot and Steinmueller (2018; 1561) framed it:

> For a decade now governments have recognised they may need to align social and environmental challenges better with innovation objectives. Climate change, reduction of inequality, poverty and pollution have been transformed into challenges and opportunities for science, technology and innovation policy.

To put it another way, the role of government is not just to facilitate economic development and correct market failures but more importantly to guide the direction of innovation towards addressing social and environmental challenges in a socially just way. As Mazzucato (2014: 24) explained, the state can play this role by investing '… in areas that the private sector would not invest even it had resources. And it is the courageous risk-taking visionary role of the state which has been ignored'. This role is different from or goes beyond tackling 'market failures' in several respects. First, it is about long-term involvement of the state in the market (and not just one-off state interventions). Second, it is about setting missions to address social and environmental challenges through innovation that is socially just. Third, it is about partnership of public and private actors to accomplish these missions and share risks and benefits.

Areas of interest to social justice, including environment and health, require research and development (R&D) spending as well as risk-taking by the state in order to generate innovative solutions. Such solutions ought not to be privately appropriated (privatised). Contemporary theorists put forward two arguments against private appropriation of innovation. The first is that innovation as such is a collective process, often supported by public funds, and therefore rewards and risks ought to be equally shared by everyone. As Ziegler (2020: 45) points out 'The idea of the heroic entrepreneur or heroic entrepreneurial organisation is ethically problematic if it legitimises a distribution of rewards that disregards contribution …'. The second argument against private appropriation of innovation is that unequal distribution of rewards and risks of new technologies is not only morally disturbing but also unsustainable. According to Mazzucato (2018: 225):

> it is crucial to understand that innovation is not a neutral concept. It can be used for different purposes – in the same way a hammer can be used to build a house or as a weapon'. Indeed, this conclusion is crucial for social justice. Depending on what is created and to whom it becomes available, innovation can worsen existing injustices or create new injustices, or it can lessen existing injustices.

For contemporary theorists of innovation and development (Mazzucato, 2014, 2021; Block and Keller, 2011), whatever emerges in terms of radical technologies involves some form of investment from the state. Therefore, the state is justified to direct these emerging technologies towards addressing societal and developmental challenges for the benefit of taxpayers. Mission oriented innovation embodies the liberal idea of distributive justice 'as reciprocity' that is founded upon the principle of proportionality of contribution. In his *A Theory of Justice*, Rawls argued that 'What a person is entitled to depends on what he does' (Rawls, 1972: 74). The interpretation of this particular argument for reciprocity is that whoever chooses not to contribute he/she cannot expect the state to sustain him/her. According to Chandler (2023: 42) Rawls's approach to reciprocity

> helps to maintain a healthy connection between contribution and reward, reflecting the underlying idea of economic justice as a form of reciprocity, where each of us makes fair contribution to the work of society in return for fair share of benefits.

Indeed, contemporary innovation theorists seem to borrow the liberal principle of reciprocity from Rawls. With focus on innovation, Ziegler (2020: 79) formulated this principle in Rawlsian terms as follows: 'Innovation processes are to be arranged in such way that they distribute the gains from innovation according to contribution'. If, as Mazzucato argues, it is the state that makes the greatest contribution to innovation through investment in visionary new areas like AI, green and health technologies, then it is the state that should receive the greatest return for its citizens. For Mazzucato (2014; 2018) as well as for Block and Keller (2011) the historical fact that for many cutting-edge innovations it has not been the invisible hand of the market that has proven decisive but the visible hand of the state, generates duties of justice.

Mazzucato (2018: 223) illustrates her argument by referring to the cases of Solyndra and Apple. As she says:

> In 2009, Solyndra, a solar-power-panel start-up received a $535 million guaranteed loan from the US Department of Energy; that same year Tesla, the electric car manufacturer, got approval for a similar loan of $465 million. In the years afterwards Tesla was widely successful and the firm repaid its loan in 2013. Solyndra, by contrast filed for bankruptcy in 2011, and among fiscal conservatives became a by words for the government's sorry track record when it comes to picking winners. Of course, if the government is to act like a venture capitalist, it will necessarily encounter many failures while earning next to nothing from success. Taxpayers footed the bill for Solyndra's losses – yet got hardly any of Tesla's profits.

This is not a desired socially just outcome. On the contrary, it privatises the rewards of Tesla's innovation success and socialises the risks of Solyndra's innovation failure, excluding the state that invested high proportion of taxpayers' money into both companies. In the case of Tesla, a desired socially just outcome could have been possible if there was, for example, a share of patents that could ensure financial rewards (and a say on the use of patents) could flow into a 'national investment fund' for future investments in new technologies (Burlamqui, 2012, Mazzucato, 2014; Ziegler, 2015).

It is clear that the liberal idea of justice as reciprocity, underpinning the combined Schumpeterian-Keynesian politics of innovation, encourages 'just desert' attached to the proportionality of some hybrid of investment-making and risk-taking. Although Mazzucato (2018: 222) is critical of the idea of 'just desert', one might argue that this is so because she seems to misunderstand it as an individual entitlement only and not as a collective one. It is true that libertarian thinkers, including Locke (1988) and Nozick (1974) approached just desert from an individualistic point of view. However, it can be argued that just desert can be applied to collectives through the state and that's in essence the implicit distributive justice argument that Mazzucato puts forward. On the basis of this argument, she wonders:

> Given the immense risks the taxpayer takes when the government invests in visionary new areas like the Internet, couldn't we construct ways for rewards from innovation to be just as social as the risks taken?

The answer appears to be straightforward positive from the perspective of justice in innovation as reciprocity. For many people, the more entrepreneurial the state becomes, the more it is justified to claim rewards from successful innovations for taxpayers. Such rewards can be regarded as the main currency of the combined Schumpeterian-Keynesian perspective of justice as reciprocity. Deficiencies of rewards from successful innovations disadvantage the citizens of the entrepreneurial state who pay their taxes.

Although the liberal idea of justice in innovation as reciprocity appeals to many people who subscribe to the entrepreneurial state argument, the problem is that it leaves out of account those who have nothing to contribute to innovation process, e.g., those who are disabled or people who don't pay taxes or individuals who abstain from any collective process of innovation and social co-operation. The question that arises is whether such people are owed anything by those who can contribute to innovation process and/or pay taxes. No obvious answer can be found in the writings of contemporary theorists who favour a combined Schumpeterian-Keynesian politics of innovation. However, this is not to suggest that theorists in the Schumpeterian and Keynesian schools of thought have not been traditionally preoccupied with questions of social welfare. In their *An Evolutionary Theory of Economic Change*, Nelson and Winter (1982: 369) argue:

> The 'gales of creative destruction' blow down the incomes not only of capitalists and managers but also of workers whose skills have become obsolete and of people who were unlucky enough to live in places where industry has become obsolete. On the other hand, this implies that compensation and rehabilitation ought to be viewed

as routine aspects of social policy in a world of rapid economic change.

This argument for social welfare, however, is not founded upon an idea of 'reciprocity' but upon a notion of 'bad luck'. In a similar way to luck egalitarians, Nelson and Winter seem to argue for compensation of bad luck. This is rather different from the argument of contemporary theorists of the entrepreneurial state who defend socialisation of benefits of innovation on the grounds of reciprocity. In contrast to Nelson and Winter, these contemporary theorists tend to favour a direction of innovation and development that might end up not taking everyone's situation and interests into account in determining what is to count as a just outcome. This is because their idea of justice in innovation as reciprocity, strictly speaking, allows only those who contribute to innovation and development process through their entrepreneurial activity and/or through their taxes to the state to receive rewards. Of course, many neo-Schumpeterian theorists would never endorse such a strict application of the idea of justice as reciprocity in innovation and development. Therefore, they would not deny that the state has a moral obligation to support people who experience disability, poverty and/or bad luck. For example, theorists such as Takala et al (2020) would defend an entrepreneurial welfare state that could tackle social issues through innovation challenge prizes and other incentives.

5.2 Hayekian Critique of Directionality

The combined Schumpeterian-Keynesian politics of innovation and development has been recently challenged by a number of neo-liberal thinkers who reconstruct Hayekian epistemological and moral arguments. Friedrich August von Hayek is widely recognised as the founding father of neo-liberalism, influencing pro-market policies of deregulation, privatisation and reduction of spending for social insurance, public health, etc. (Papaioannou, 2012). Although he never explicitly wrote on innovation and development, he formulated an epistemologically founded critique of central economic planning and defended the neo-liberal idea of the market as a spontaneous order. In his work on *Collectivist Economic Planning* in 1935 and later in his *The Road to Serfdom* in 1944 and in his Individualism and Economic Order in 1948, Hayek argued for the impossibility of central economic planning, drawing on the socialist calculation debate, and raising the issue of limited knowledge. For him, the knowledge required by policy makers to make central planning work would never be assembled. Central planning is inefficient and ignores the role of market competition as a discovery procedure. It is this procedure that leads to innovation, involving individual entrepreneurs the actions of which produce unintended consequences, including new process and technological products.

In the Hayekian perspective, innovation and development cannot be possibly planned (i.e. big I innovation and big D development) let alone be directed centrally by the state. This is due to limited knowledge of policy makers who are unable to understand the complexity of innovation and development process and the market institutions. All the state can end up doing is coercing entrepreneurs and development practitioners to move to specific directions and hence limiting their individual freedom. This creates a moral issue on top of the epistemological problem. In his *The Constitution of Liberty*, Hayek (1960: 12) conceives freedom as 'an absence of coercion'. According to him:

> By coercion we mean such a control of the environment or circumstances of a person by another that, in order to avoid greater evil, he is forced to act not according to a coherent plan of his own but to serve the ends of another.
>
> (Hayek, 1960: 20–21)

This conception is in line with Isaiah Berlin's liberal notion of freedom as the absence of any 'deliberate interference of other human beings within the area in which I could otherwise act' (Berlin, 1975: 34). The area within which individual entrepreneurs act is the market that ought to be free in negative terms (free from state interference). In Hayekian terms, freedom implies that the state ought to have very limited role in directing entrepreneurial activity and innovations towards specific objectives and/or mission, e.g., addressing societal challenges such as health, climate change, poverty and inequality.

In Hayek's theory, liberal economic institutions such as the free market and the system of prices come about spontaneously as undesigned mechanisms of knowledge diffusion (that in many respects is tacit and individuals are not aware of having such knowledge). Clearly this theory has impact on the notion of innovation and development. If knowledge can be mainly generated through the engagement of individual entrepreneurs in the market, then innovation let alone development depend on the unintended consequences of market competition and not on state investment in cutting edge technologies and developmental projects. In fact, the Hayekian perspective is that the state does not have any role to play in directing innovation and development towards social justice. Hayek's *The Road to Serfdom* was an epistemological and moral critique of all forms of Keynesianism and collectivism which contemplated interference with the spontaneous order of the market (and inevitably, innovation). Hayek (1973: 36) defined order as:

> a state of affairs in which a multiplicity of elements of various kinds are so related to each other that we may learn from our acquaintance with some spatial or temporal part of the whole to form correct expectations concerning the rest or at least expectations which have a good chance of proving correct.

This definition clearly raises the problem of knowing the whole of complex orders such as the market and the innovation and development processes. Accepting spontaneity and uncertainty is Hayek's solution to the epistemological and moral problem of state interference with these complex orders.

Contemporary theorists of innovation and development who question the combined Schumpeterian-Keynesian politics of the entrepreneurial and developmental state (Wennberg and Sandström, 2022; Davidson and Potts, 2022; Murtina et al, 2022; Karlson et al, 2021; Potts, 2018; Mingardi, 2015) draw on this Hayekian definition of spontaneous order to warn us that '… what may sound good on paper in terms of collective missions and directionality are often – but not always – at odds with the received wisdom of individual action and co-ordination in open democratic societies' (Wennberg and Sandström, 2022: 3). For them, such coordination ought to be within the spontaneous order of the market. Therefore, they accuse proponents of the combined Schumpeterian-Keynesian politics of innovation and development of ignoring the limits of human knowledge and the importance of spontaneity for co-ordination in open democratic societies.

Defenders of Hayekian politics of innovation and development also dismiss the argument for the entrepreneurial state as partisan and shaky in terms of historical evidence. For instance, Karlson et al (2021) provide a historical review of entrepreneurial state policies in

Sweden such as direct public support to innovation (e.g. government grants) and indirect subsidies (e.g. R&D tax credits), insisting that such innovation policies are often exaggerated and that outcomes in terms new technologies and growth have been disappointing. On the other hand, Worstall (2013) contests the entrepreneurial state argument on the grounds that technological innovation is not a public good and therefore the government is not morally justified to interfere with the process through policies of research and development (R&D). In a similar manner, Mingardi (2015: 608) argues that '…in many respects it [the entrepreneurial state argument] suffers from the "is-ought" problem – that is, it makes too many claims about what we ought to be based on statements of what is'. He therefore accuses Schumpeterian-Keynesian theorists and especially Mazzucato, for developing arbitrary arguments, overemphasising 'a tiny bit of history' of the 20th century and failing to provide a holistic historical perspective, including the 19th-century industrialisation that was independent of huge public investment in R&D. In short, Mingardi regards the entrepreneurial state theory as ideological and biased towards a strong public sector. However, analysing his argument, one might also brand it as ideological, suffering from exactly the same problem: lack of historical evidence. Mingardi's only counter historical examples are focused on the Industrial Revolution, e.g., railways, failing to accept the fact that involvement of the state has been key for setting up collaborative knowledge and innovation ecosystems that delivered new technologies as both intended and unintended consequences of industrial policy. Overemphasising the role of the market and dismissing the historical importance of state industrial policy are rather unconvincing strategies for defeating the combined Schumpeterian-Keynesian politics.

Although it is true that this politics of innovation and development implies businesses take less risk than the state, it is also true that the latter has more substantial involvement in early stages of technological invention than the former. As Block (2018: 29) suggests in his *Capitalism: The Future of an Illusion*

> within the parameters of an economy with private ownership and the pursuit of profitability, there is still very wide leeway to decide how large or small a role the state will play, how much inequality will be tolerated, and how deep and broad democratic governance will be.

Block's suggestion is a clear response to Hayekians such as Mingardi who tend to see the market economy as being free, coherent and above all a spontaneous order that has its own dynamics. This view of the market fails to understand the micro-level technology development and the role of the state policy in stimulating innovation. In fact, there is no such thing as a market order for setting priorities in technology. Visionary and strategic political choices have to be made by governments. As Ziegler (2020: 122) also notes 'In spite of the evolutionary language often used in entrepreneurial research, innovation is not blind, natural force but something strategically pursued and fostered …' that can still have unintended consequences for people and the environment. For example, the strategic pursuit of technologies such as pesticides and fertilisers for the so-called Green Revolution had tremendous impact on soil and water quality, given that these chemicals have long-lasting effect on environment.

Hayekian theorists of innovation and development aim to leave governments out of the process of directing innovation towards addressing grand developmental challenges from a justice perspective. One reason for that is the epistemological limitations of innovation and development policy. According to Sandström and Alm (2022: 235):

> Generally, calls for increased directionality are made without limitations of policy or policy making. Evidence of policy failure is scarcely reviewed, yet there are, by now, many studies pointing out the limited effects of more interventionist policy approaches and support structures aiming to raise innovation summarised extant evidence on government interventions for innovation: 'for each effective government intervention, there have been dozens, even hundreds, of failures where substantial public expenditures bore no fruit'.

Sandström and Alm insist that only the discovery procedure of free competition can select stronger technologies through trial and error. This process is neutral and impartial, preventing the state from picking up winners. It might be argued that neutrality and impartiality are key pillars of the neo-liberal idea of justice in innovation underpinning Hayekian politics. Hayek himself called this idea of justice as 'commutative justice' that '…takes no account of personal or subjective circumstances of needs or good intentions, but solely how the results of man's activities are valued by those who make use of them' (Hayek, 1967: 257).

The Hayekian idea of commutative justice implies that only the impartial and neutral process of the market can deliver just outcomes in terms of distributing innovation rewards and risks. These rewards and risks are not merely resources to be distributed. As Ziegler (2020) points out, abstracting from relational rewards and risks conceals numerous directly justice-relevant questions about inequalities to be dealt with in the process of innovation. However, it is clear this idea of justice in innovation and development excludes those who are unable to participate in the competitive market process. From this it follows that the poor could never get the chance to value certain cutting-edge and expensive innovations because they could never get the chance to buy them and make use of them. Although many Hayekian theorists do not necessarily favour strict application of commutative justice and therefore, they support limited policies of poverty relief so that everybody can participate in the consumption of innovations, these policies might be insufficient to give the poor purchasing power.

But even if the poor could somehow get the chance to buy and make use of such expensive innovations, they would not necessarily enter relations of social equality with the rich due to issues of exploitation, domination, hierarchy and oppression which, sometimes, are independent of equal distribution of rewards of innovation. Imagine two persons (Person A = Female and Person B = Male) who receive the same reward for a successful innovation (e.g. a new digital technology). This material equality cannot eliminate the possibility for a Person A to dominate and oppress Person B (and the reverse) because of non-material or non-economic factors in play (e.g. cultural and/or religious norms, exercise of physical or psychological power, etc.). These issues would persist unless a relational justice was in place to identify them in detail and then try to mitigate them in non-ideal terms (i.e. mitigate them), directing innovation towards just outcomes. It might be argued that the neo-liberal idea of commutative justice in innovation that the Hayekians favour, tends to suffer from the same theoretical ills that the liberal idea of justice in innovation as reciprocity suffers, i.e., overwhelmingly focuses on resources ignoring inequality of relations in the process of generation and diffusion of new technologies. Yet, as I am arguing in the next section, innovation policy ought to prioritise inequality of relations and try to mitigate it through targeted interventions in order to deliver (non-ideal) just outcomes.

5.3 The Relational Way Forward

As has been shown in this chapter, despite differences, both the combined Schumpeterian-Keynesian and the Hayekian theoretical camps rely on liberal or neo-liberal notions of morality and politics which tend to justify predominantly distributional currencies of justice. These currencies of justice include resources such as income and wealth. Of course, these resources matter enormously because they influence who is able to appropriate the material benefits of innovation and development. At the same time, the almost exclusive focus on material resources seems to be overlooking questions of relational equality in the process of generation and diffusion of new technologies. The liberal principle of reciprocity justifies 'desert' for those who have proportionately contributed to innovation more than others. It differs from the neo-liberal principle of commutative justice which rejects 'desert' on epistemological and moral grounds, and instead justifies rewards determined by the free market competition. The latter might potentially reward nothing to those who have contributed to innovations but have failed to sell them in the market making profit. However, both principles are focused on distribution and in this sense, they fail to go far enough to mitigate unjust relations of domination, exploitation, oppression, and hierarchies within processes of production and diffusion of novel technologies and goods (e.g. IPRs) for development. Such relations are in essence power relations, i.e., relations of control of social actors over others (e.g. innovators, regulators, publics, etc.). They have been constructed historically of different scales within national and global innovation systems and require agency and public action to be changed.

As has been repeatedly argued in this book, justice in innovation and development ought to be predominantly relational, not only distributional. A relational theory of social justice in innovation and development presupposes a level of equal distribution of risks and rewards that is not absolute and therefore allows for marginal profit incentives of entrepreneurship to be maintained. Although such incentives are not the only ones in play when it comes to major innovations based on scientific breakthroughs, this theory considers them to be important within market societies. Marginal incentives for innovators to produce marginally more than they would otherwise would, can unlock growth that facilitates equalisation of relations between members of society. However, if such growth becomes unequal to the extent that the gap between worst-off and better-off threatens equality of relations, then the state is justified to intervene to close this gap.

As has been stressed in Chapters 1 and 2, theory of justice holds that each member of society ought to stand in equal relations to other members of society. It draws on proponents of social equalitarianism such as Anderson (1999) and Scheffler (2005, 2015) who have criticised the distributive notion of egalitarianism that holds that each member of society ought to enjoy equal share of the society's resources, including rewards of innovation. They have also defended a non-ideal notion of relational justice. Clearly, absolute equal share of the society's resources, including innovative technologies, may be not required equality of relations. What this suggests is that equality of relations requires a relative equal share of the society's resources. In a fully just society (from a relational equalitarian perspective) all people would have broadly access to resources they need to relate equally to one another.

Proponents of the competing approach of distributive equalitarianism such as Cohen (1989), Arneson (2004), and Dworkin (2000, 1981) have faced questions about their ideal principles of freedom and equality, as well as accusations of ignoring the politically oppressed, the relational inequalities of race, class and caste, and the victims of genocide and slavery (Anderson, 1999). These issues of injustice are at the heart of innovation and development. As such, innovation and development are about technological and socio-economic changes which create opportunities for addressing injustices but also pose risks of exacerbating them (Buchanan et al, 2011). According to social equalitarians, these risks are not a matter of undeserved bad luck (the impact of which needs to be eliminated) but rather a matter of unequal oppressive relations in society. It follows that the point of equality in innovation is not primarily distributional but relational. This implies that we start off with systematic identification of relational inequalities and then we move on to explain some of them through identification of causes (e.g. distributional inequalities, gender biases, race discrimination, etc.).

The case of emerging technologies confirms the following: for innovation to embrace relations of equality, it must prevent people from entering superior-inferior relations in the process of knowledge generation, knowledge exploitation and technological change (Papaioannou, 2021). Such relations, whether they be marginalisation (e.g. of certain geographies in the Global South and/or excluded publics), hierarchy (e.g. scientists and technical experts versus practitioners), domination (e.g. scientific knowledge versus traditional knowledge) and exploitation (e.g. exploitative relations between companies and scientists), have no place in innovative and developmental communities of equals. As argued elsewhere, such communities are free and democratic in the sense that innovators, regulators, and users of technology are not in coercive relations of hierarchy with one another, but in relations of equality. Relations of equality in innovation and development need to be protected from unjustified asymmetries of knowledge, undeserved inequalities of resources (e.g. unequal diffusion of benefits of innovation) deprivation of human capabilities, post-colonial dependencies and exclusions.

However, it needs to be stressed again that such relations of equality are not absolute. If there are justified asymmetries of knowledge (e.g. some persons make a free choice to research more than others and therefore to generate more knowledge than others on specific topics of interest) and deserved inequalities of resources and capabilities (e.g. some persons make a choice to spend less resources on satisfying expensive tastes and instead invest more in developing their central capabilities), then relations of equality in innovation and development are relative. The question that arises is this: what is the threshold above which such distributional inequalities become morally unjustified and threaten for an innovative and developmental society of equals?

As an answer to this question, it might be argued that prioritising relational equality over distributional equality of resources in innovation and development implies that maximisation of profit is morally justified and accepted only so long as it does not cause minimisation of relational equality, e.g., creating oppressive or exclusive relations between innovators, regulators, and publics. This proposed threshold is in line with Moles and Parr (2019) argument that, in fact, distributive egalitarianism and social egalitarianism are mutually supportive in a range of cases. Both aspects of justice (distributional and relational) are important (but insufficient on their own). In other words, as Schemmel (2011) suggests, given that relational egalitarians are committed to a co-operative society of equals, they ought to accept that there are reasons of justice in favour of limiting distributive inequality in socially produced goods, e.g., innovative technologies.

Indeed, in significant cases of innovation and development, the distributive and the social equalitarian ethos work together to deliver just outcome. Thus, for example, when it comes to elimination of poverty and hunger or to achievement of quality education and gender equality (SDGs 1-5) we have strong reasons to secure for each member of society equal share of basic resources in order to ensure each member of society stands the chance of escaping poverty, receiving equal level of quality education and taking equal opportunities regardless of gender, race, culture, etc. To put it another way, in almost all significant cases of innovation (e.g. the Internet, AI, green technologies, life sciences, etc.), we have reasons to distribute resources simply because we have reasons to ensure certain relations between innovators, regulators and publics. As Moles and Parr (2019: 137) point out '… our concern for these kinds of relations also provides grounds upon which to object to highly unequal distributions or resources, even if no one is in particular badly off'. Highly unequal distribution of resources such as ML and AI technologies in sectors, including food, energy and medicines within countries, might be objected on the grounds of relational equality they cause.

Within countries, traditional Keynesian politics has tried to deal with inequality through a conception of welfare state. Since the end of World War II, this modern state has funded an adequate education system, social insurance and pensions, public health care, etc. It has done so through a particular mechanism of distributing resources (e.g. rewards of innovation), including income tax, corporation tax and value added tax (VAT). However, recent data (UNCTAD, 2021) reveals that within country inequality is on the rise again. This trend includes both developed countries such as the United States and the European Union and developing countries such as China and India. Although dominance of Hayekian politics promoting the market (as opposed redistribution of resources through the welfare state) is one part of the explanation of rising within country inequality, technological innovation is the other part. The installation and deployment periods of new technologies such as digital technologies, big data, robotics, AI, drones, and the Internet of Things (IoT) are uneven (Perez, 2002) generating winners and losers within countries. According to UNCTAD (2021) these technologies already represent a $350-billion market and one that could grow to $3.2 trillion by 2025.

In order to establish equal relations within countries, distributional inequality of resources should be limited to morally acceptable threshold. The morally acceptable threshold of distributional inequality of resources (e.g. rewards of innovation) is a threshold that does not cause unequal relations of domination and oppression within and between countries. To paraphrase Rawls' difference principle: distributional inequalities are just if and only if they're part of an arrangement that maintains relations of equality between all members of society. To put it another way, the legitimation of marginal distributional inequality of resources such as rewards of innovation, depends on the extent to which this maintains relations of equality between all members of society, including the innovators, the regulators, and the publics. Increase of distributional inequality above the threshold leads to creation of unequal relations of domination, oppression, and exploitation between people. Therefore, distributional inequality ceases to be marginal and no longer constitutes an incentive of innovation. It's at this point that the state is morally justified to intervene to rectify relational justice through reduction of distributional inequality to a morally acceptable threshold.

Innovation can be politically directed towards social justice provided politics adopts what I outlined as relational theory of justice. This theory accepts that a marginal threshold of distributional inequality of resources can incentivise the profit drive of innovation without jeopardising equality of relations. No other inequality is justified in innovation. Narratives about innovators taking high risks and therefore deserving high rewards are not in line with the relational justice in innovation outlined above.

Now the question that arises is what sort of politics can direct innovation and development towards delivering just outcomes from a relational perspective, given the inability of Schumpeterian-Keynesian politics and Hayekian politics to move beyond distributional concerns about innovation and development. In previous works (Papaioannou, 2018, 2016, 2014) I have argued that liberal state politics is not necessarily the best way to achieve directionality in innovation and development. This is not only because of capacity and legitimacy issues of states but also because of the fact that, as a recent UNRISD (2022: 14) report points out:

> There are sufficient data to suggest that political systems bent towards the preferences of elites … Elites wield influence over policies and legislation through various strategies, including influencing the electoral process through business networks and lobbying, media control or outright state capture.

UNRISD in essence confirms Wright's recent diagnosis and critique of liberal democracy that, according to him, it is unable '... to insulate political decision-making from the exercise of power connected to capitalist wealth' (Wright, 2012: 7).

This implies, for example, that an entrepreneurial state intending for Schumpeterian-Keynesian politics can be easily highjacked by lobbying groups representing the narrow interests of multinational companies (e.g. energy giants, big pharmaceuticals, etc.) and directing innovation towards unjust outcomes. More transparency and participation regarding the decisions of entrepreneurial state would be possible with greater engagement of publics. The conditions of such engagement include: education, time and resources. Yet the entrepreneurial state appears to be centralised and unable to meet transparency and participatory requirements of innovation (Papaioannou, 2021). Indeed, as Ziegler (2020: 83) notes:

> These transparency and participatory requirements might slow-down the pace of change, but if the reason for the slow-down is greater consideration with a view to improving benefits to the least advantaged, then the slow-down in such cases is part of innovation for justice.

In fact, lack of transparency and participatory governance can open the door to an authoritarian entrepreneurial state (Papaioannou, 2021) that can potentially shut down bottom-up (pluralist) innovation alternatives to illegitimate missions (also see Stirling, 2024; Fortuny-Sicart and Pansera, 2024). Mazzucato (2021) defends the role of the entrepreneurial state in making bets and picking winners and directions of innovation and development which promise to accomplish specific missions. Such missions can dictate the direction of change towards technologies for private good. Hence, this top-down political approach can potentially suppress bottom-up alternatives. Centralised states and their missions have historically been vulnerable to failures of democratic accountability. Their exercise of state power could not be subordinated to power of civil societies. There is no reason why the entrepreneurial state would be an exemption to this historical legacy of centralised states within capitalism. In fact, a number of Middle Eastern regimes, e.g., Saudi Arabia and United Arab Emirates (UAE) have been operating as authoritarian entrepreneurial states, pursuing missions such as developing green economy infrastructures and investing in smart city technologies. Their top-down approaches reinforce the argument that Mazzucato's theory of the entrepreneurial state is compatible with or at least vulnerable to authoritarianism in certain developmental contexts. At the end of the day, as DeGraaff et al (2025) point out, policy directions of the state are political, reflecting beliefs and ideologies of dominant actors around direction.

Instead of state politics, I have suggested that public action and campaigning for just innovation and development can push for the rectification of relational injustices, ensuring directionality of technologies that is morally acceptable. The politics of public action and campaigning is predominantly bottom up, involving participation of various marginalised groups. Take for example, public actions and campaigns for the so-called grassroots or below the radar innovation. As has been explained earlier in the book, these are actions and campaigns by low-and-middle income groups which draw on indigenous knowledge to introduce low tech innovations which tend to equalise social relations within communities. For example, the introduction of a low-cost prosthetic leg to poor persons facing disability enables them to relate more equally to others and their communities, participating in activities they would not be able to participate otherwise. The introduction of micro-credit options to the bottom of the pyramid (BoP) of global income distribution (i.e. the income-poor) challenges the dominant idea of banking that is exclusive of the income-poor and improves equality in terms of relations with non-income poor (i.e. middle-and-high people). The same holds for other grassroots innovations ranging from community support agriculture and eco-housing to complementary currencies and credit unions (Smith and Sterling, 2018).

The common denominator of public actions and campaigns for grassroots or below the radar innovations is their counter-hegemonic character. Such actions and campaigns are very much political, challenging domination by powerful market companies, putting forwards an alternative direction of innovation and towards freedom and sustainability. According to UNRISD (2022: 25)

> New forms of collaboration are emerging among marginalised groups as the apply various strategies to adapt to rapidly changing environments while stabilising their livelihoods. They develop innovative strategies to increase their capital base for investments

> … or co-produce social services as a way to change their relations with state and market providers, for example, in the case of informal workers in India and Thailand.

Indeed, UNRISD research confirms that the politics of public action and campaigning, inspired by ideas of relational justice and common good, putting pressure from below, can go long way towards more just and sustainable approaches (UNRISD, 2022). Such approaches embrace pluralism of innovative activity across a variety market and non-market contexts. This implies a direction towards what Wright (2010, 2012) theorised as 'real utopias', namely, bottom-up configurations of innovation which are facilitated by politics of collective agency to deliver just outcomes. Although 'real utopias' are not radical in the sense of suggesting the overthrow of capitalism through revolution, they are pragmatic in the sense of proposing the gradual consolidation of schemes of equal co-operation.

Unequal social relations through which people marginalise others can be changed through this politics of collective agency, including campaigns and public actions of grassroots innovation movements (Smith et al, 2017). A non-ideal theory of justice in innovation should subscribe to pragmatism in line with politics of public action to enable transformative change. Public action as such emerges when empirical identification and causal explanation of injustice raises the question of '… what can and ought to be done about it, and who should be charged with correcting it' (Anderson, 2010: 22). Indeed, as Harvey (1992) also points out, social mobilisation and organisation are driven by bottom-up claims of social justice. Such claims are relational (not just distributional) and require both evaluation and attribution of political responsibility for change (Harvey, 1992). In terms of evaluation, it might be argued that judgements about relational injustices in innovation can be based on normative reflections which are both historically and socially contextualised. This is what Young (1990: 5) regards as 'critical theory'. In her view, 'Critical theory presumes that normative ideals used to criticise society are rooted in experience of and reflection on that very society, and that norms can come from nowhere else'.

The main principles of relational justice in innovation and development which I have discussed in Chapter 2 (i.e. equity, recognition, and participation) are in line with Young's critical theory. This is because they emerge from the bottom-up through reflection on that very process of generating new knowledge and technological solutions to problems of society and economy.

These principles are embodied in the everyday discourse about justice in innovation and development. As Young (1990: 5) clarifies:

> these are not theorems to be demonstrated in a self-enclosed system. They are instead calls, pleas, claims upon some people by others. Relational reflection on justice begins by a hearing, in heeding a call, rather than in asserting and mastering a state of affairs, however ideal. The call to 'be just' is always situated in concrete social and political practices that precede and exceed the philosopher.

By contesting relations of power, domination and oppression, public activists generate egalitarian principles of justice in innovation which are not necessarily liberal and tend to go beyond distribution of benefits of innovation and towards equalisation of social relations.

5.4 Concluding Remarks

This chapter has sought to evaluate two political approaches to innovation and development directionality towards just outcomes. On the one hand, a combined Schumpeterian-Keynesian politics that puts forward the idea of justice in innovation and development as reciprocity; namely people deserve just rewards from successful innovations and developmental outcomes according to the proportion of their contribution to innovation and development processes. On the other hand, a Hayekian politics that puts forward the idea of justice in innovation and development as a commutative process: namely people deserve to receive rewards from successful innovations and development projects on the grounds of how the free market values their innovative and developmental activities.

I have argued that both approaches to directionality of innovation and development are predominantly ideal and distributional, failing to appreciate the primacy of relational justice. Therefore, they also fail to mitigate oppressive relations and hierarchies in the process of generation and diffusion of new technologies. I have insisted that for innovation and development to be directed towards just outcomes, the approach should be relational. This implies that we ought to prioritise relational equality over equality of material resources. Of course, certain level of equality of material resources is presupposed of equality of social relations. However, equality of material resources cannot be absolute but relative to its impact on equality of social relations. This leaves us with some space for inequality in innovation and development that can function as an incentive and/or benefit for everyone, so long as it does not cause unequal social relations of domination and oppression in the generation and diffusion of new technologies.

The main policy implications of a relational theory of justice in innovation and development are twofold. First, bottom-up calls and claims of inequality in the process of knowledge generation and exploitation need to be systematically investigated by policy makers. Secondly, identified issues of relational injustice need to be addressed through non-ideal 'trial and error' measures which neither disincentivise innovators nor exclude public activists and campaigners from the political decision-making process on the direction of innovation and development. Public action and campaigning for justice in innovation are crucial for directing new technologies towards building a society of equals.

Note

1 For example, many Hayekians support redistributive policies where everybody gets access to some level of income and public service. In this sense, they contradict the ideal of catallaxy as a spontaneous order that peacefully delivers benefits to everyone without the need of state intervention. Similarly, Keynesians support pro-market policies of free competition and limited welfare state in order to allow for incentives of entrepreneurial activity.

6 The Role of the State

What kind of political state is able to take forward the relational approach to directionality of innovation and development? In the 21st century, the notion of the political state and its (positive or negative) role in innovation and development have become dominant topics of theoretical and empirical inquiry. The state is broadly defined as '… a single, unified source of political authority for a territory, drawing upon the undivided loyalties of its population, operating in a well-organised and permanent way, and directed towards the interests of the whole society' (Dryzek and Dunleavy, 2009: 2). Yet, this broad definition is exclusive; it does not consider the historical fact that the political state as such is neither a unitary subject nor a smooth apparatus of political authority. Instead, as the Greek political sociologist Nicos Poulantzas (1978) insisted, the state is an institutional ensemble which mobilises consent vis-à-vis the dominated classes in society and organises the hegemony within the power bloc of dominating classes. This institutional ensemble of the state suffers from internal contradictions and conflicts. Certainly, as Skinner (1989) has shown, the character of the state is impersonal. This means that it is distinct from its rulers but also from the ruled. Features of the modern state include: governing institutions, collectively binding decision-making, monopoly of legitimate use of force, sovereignty and clear distinction between public and private realms of activity (Skinner, 1989).

As has been already shown, theorists such as Block (2008), Block and Keller (2011), Mazzucato (2014) and many others have argued that the state has been crucial for promoting innovation and technological change. They are right. In fact, even within neo-liberal institutional settings like those of the United States (US) and the United

DOI: 10.4324/9781003652083-7

Kingdom (UK), the state has managed to perform a hidden developmental role that delivered investments in innovative technologies, including the Internet and the iPhone. Although, as has been stressed, innovation theorists clearly unpack the myth of free market fundamentalism[1] in industrial policy and practice of neo-liberal states, they don't fully explain how precisely such states have been justified and legitimised to have extensive roles in economy and society. More importantly, they don't admit the fact that these hidden developmental states still reproduce a social division of labour that is exploitative, delivering most benefits to a power bloc of dominant classes, including bourgeoisie classes, and leaving powerless classes behind, including working classes and other disadvantaged communities. The values and positions of a power bloc (that represents the unity of several fractions under the leadership of one dominant fraction that claims to promote the same interests as capital) tend to be privileged by research and development (R&D) driven innovation over other less powerful classes including, working classes. Therefore, democracy is limited (Smith and Sterling, 2018) and social justice cannot be achieved in the diffusion of new technologies.

The question that arises is, in essence, what is the role of the state in innovation and development? Is the role of the state to reproduce unequal and exploitative social relations of innovation and economic growth via the social division of labour or is the role of the state to promote equality of social relations and inclusion via a reconciliation of social divisions in production of novel goods and services? To answer this question, there is a need for more in depth and critical theorisation of the state than that of contemporary innovation and development theorists. Putting forward a plausible political argument about the innovation and development state presupposes proper understanding of the state as such. To satisfy this need, Poulantzas' theory of the state will be revisited. Unfortunately, this theory is absent from the current theorising of the state by innovation and development thinkers. This absence is particularly noticeable in academic books and articles which are preoccupied with institutional approaches to technical and technological change. They ignore the political state as a social relation.

This chapter insists that contemporary innovation and development theorists can learn a lot from the politico-sociological arguments of Poulantzas. Although his arguments have received criticism over the years for their structuralist foundations (Miliband, 1970; Laclau, 1975; Block, 1987), their advantage remains twofold: first Poulantzas conceives the state as a result of the social division of labour and therefore acknowledges the unity between politics and economics; second, he considers the state to be a condensation of conflicting social relations which have their own materiality and therefore does not abstract from the historical limitations of capitalism. However, despite advantages, Poulantzas' theory faces its own limitations. The most important of them is that it offers just one alternative to capitalist innovation and development state, i.e., democratic socialism. Yet there may be other alternatives too, emerging from the bottom up, especially in the global South. To grasp them, we need to move beyond Poulantzas' structuralism and towards embracing pluralism and the role of public action in social change.

In what follows, the argument of this chapter will be developed in three sections. Section 6.1 revisits Poulantzas' theory of the state. Section 6.2 attempts to go beyond Poulantzas, arguing that the role of the state is to emancipate itself from the social division of labour and promote (non-exploitative) social co-operation, producing just outcomes. Section 6.3 discusses bottom-up initiatives of innovation and development. Section 6.4 concludes by summarising the main argument of this paper.

6.1 Revisiting Poulantzas' Theory of the State

The 21st-century state is (and ought to be) concerned about innovation and development, especially their positive and negative consequences. This is so for all the reasons which Bush (1945) explained in his *Science, the Endless Frontier*, including economic growth, employment, public health, and natural security. For Bush, all the things that innovation and development help us achieve are the very objectives of government. However, innovation and development are not only important for economic growth and employment, but also for social justice (Papaioannou, 2020; Papaioannou and Srinivas, 2019). This chapter has taken an egalitarian perspective of justice, focusing primarily on social relations instead of resources such as economic growth. From this perspective, innovation and development can create favourable conditions for achieving social justice or pose risks of injustice, i.e., making some people worse off or exacerbating their disadvantaged positions (Papaioannou, 2018; Buchanan et al, 2011). In relational terms, the latter might translate into making some people more exploited or oppressed than others.

Economists, innovation theorists, and political scientists tend to provide rather competing accounts of innovation and development state. Some of these accounts are explicit while some others are implicit. However, they tend to ignore Poulantzas' theory of the state. This theory puts forward an alternative notion of the state as a social relation that has the potential to organise the transition from capitalism to democratic socialism.

At first glance, of course, the discussion of Poulantzas' theory of the state in innovation and development studies in general and in this book in particular might seem irrelevant for a number of reasons. First, Poulantzas never used the term 'innovation state' or 'developmental state'. Second, his references to innovation and development are in passing and always inside the advanced capitalist states. Poulantzas is interested in the relationship between knowledge and power, particularly the way in which scientists '... have become state functionaries ...' (Poulantzas, 1974: 57). Thirdly, he is mainly a theorist of capitalist formations.

However, I argue that the discussion of Poulantzas' theory is important from an explanatory perspective. In contrast to theorists of innovation state, he is a Marxist thinker who developed a broad political theory of the state drawing on Gramsci's notion of hegemony, i.e., the exercise of intellectual, moral, and political leadership by the ruling class to achieve the successful reproduction of 'active consent' of dominated groups. Like Marx and Engels, Gramsci understood the state as a result of the capitalist division of labour and hence the further division of society into social classes. The persistence of such divisions are directly related to the state's existence. In return, the state does everything it can to maintain and reproduce the capitalist division of labour and social classes. Gramsci extended the Marxian theory of the state to include private organisations of civil society, including the church, the schools, the universities, the press, the mass media, etc., responsible for spreading hegemonic ideologies of the capitalist state.

Poulantzas took Gramsci's theory of the state and civil society forward, highlighting the relational aspects of this complex apparatus. He developed Gramsci's autonomy of spheres of superstructure, namely, political and civil society (Coutinho, 2012). Poulantzas also agreed that this superstructure is nothing more than the ensemble of social relations of production within capitalism. According to Jessop (1982: 153): '

> Poulantzas is the single most influential Marxist political theorist of the post-war period and, up to his premature death in 1979 he produced a significant body of work on the capitalist state.

Jessop provided a magisterial survey of Poulantzas' theoretical development and his notion of the state. This work suggests that Poulantzas elaborated the state as a relation between socio-economic forces. Indeed, in his *State, Power, and Socialism*, he argued that

> The (capitalist) State should not be regarded as an intrinsic entity: like 'capital' it is rather a relationship of forces, or more precisely the material condensation of such relationship between classes and class fractions, such as this is expressed within the state in a necessarily specific form.
>
> (Poulantzas, 1974: 128)

This argument reflects Poulantzas' concern with the class nature of the state and the historical fact that it privileges some agents over others. However, the actualisation of such state biases towards specific agents is relative to the changing balance of forces, strategies and tactics within the state apparatus (Jessop, 2016).

In his reply to Miliband and Laclau's critiques of his theory, Poulantzas explains that '… the term 'relative' in the expression 'relative autonomy' of the state (relative in relation to what and to whom?) *here* refers to the relationship between state and dominant classes (i.e. relatively autonomous in relation to the dominant classes). In other words, it refers to the class struggle within each social formation and to its corresponding state forms' (Poulantzas, 1976: 72). However, Poulantzas stresses that the degree of autonomy of the state varies across different contexts and historical forms of the state. For example, the state in Europe might be thought as more autonomous than the state in the US. The bottom line for Poulantzas is this:

> conceiving of the capitalist state as a relation, as being structurally shot through and constituted with and by class contradictions, means firmly grasping the fact that an institution (the state) that is destined to reproduce class divisions cannot be monolithic fissure less bloc, but is itself by virtue of its very structure divided. The various organs and branches of the state (ministries and government offices, executive and parliament, central administration and

> local and regional authorities, army, judiciary, etc) reveal major contradictions among themselves.
>
> (Poulantzas, 1976)

In essence, these contradictions explain why the state can maintain some relative autonomy from dominant classes when it comes to actual policymaking. Non-Marxist theorists such as Skocpol (2008) also recognise so, emphasising the state capacity to take autonomous decisions and design policies which are not always reducible to class interests.

Although Poulantzas is not an innovation or developmental state theorist, his explanatory account of the capitalist state has implications for both innovation and development, let alone related public policies. These implications should be taken seriously by contemporary innovation and development theorists. First, the capitalist state can set up a system of innovation and intervene in the market to support the competitive advantage of domestic firms and hence to promote local and national economic development. Even though illiberal, since the 1980s, the capitalist innovation and development state has operated within what Schot and Steinmueller (2016: 9) have characterised as 'Framing 2: National Systems of Innovation'. Indeed, the very concept of the system of innovation became popular among academics and development policymakers during that decade, even though, as Godin (2020) observes, it goes back to the 1960s. The reason of this popularity was that the concept of systems of innovation enabled a holistic policy approach to innovation and development that concerned several ministries and public agencies of the capitalist state. Despite the neo-liberal rhetoric of the 1980s, the capitalist state used its autonomy to construct intervention policies of innovation (e.g. measures for economic environment, taxation, trade, etc.). It did so to satisfy the desire of dominant classes for more dynamic capital accumulation. The state in the 2020s might do the same, leading what Schot and Steinmueller (Godin, 2020) have defined as 'Framing 3: Transformative Change'. Within this framing, innovation is politically directed to address challenges such as climate change, reduction of equality, poverty, and pollution.

Second, the relations and contradictions within the capitalist state are the direct result of the social division of labour. The latter '... expresses itself in the presence of the political and ideological relations within the production process, which has primacy over the technical division of labour' (Poulantzas, 1978: 35). This implies that the capitalist innovation and development state embodies oppressive and exploitative relations of production. Such relations are at the core of unjust and exclusive technological innovations which promote development for dominant social classes, marginalising the rest. What matters is not so much the technical division of labour that leads to certain technologies (e.g. iPhone, GPS, etc.) but the relational context and the unjust structures within which such technologies emerge. Often such context is not just exploitative but also gendered and racialised. Overlooking the importance of this context can give the wrong impression that innovation is a natural activity driven predominantly by technical rationality and has nothing to do with the structures of politics of the capitalist state. Yet innovation is very much political, depending on the social division of labour that the capitalist state promotes. As Freeman and Soete (1997) show in their third edition of *The Economics of Industrial Innovation*, the generation but also the acceptability of innovative products and processes is very much conditioned by politics. The developmental impact of innovation is also political in the sense that it involves politics in order to be realised.

Contemporary innovation and development theorists tend to emphasise the external role of the state in R&D investments and in technological missions. For example, in her book *Mission Economy: A Moonshot Guide to Changing Capitalism*, Mazzucato (2021) considers the state to be a value creator that can be driven by public purpose to provide directions towards more inclusive and sustainable capitalism. Mazzucato defines public value as whatever is legitimately created by the state or government on behalf of the public (Collington and Mazzucato, 2022). In this sense, she argues that services and goods traditionally produced by the state to add value to the public cannot be outsourced to the private sector. Instead, the private sector should be co-ordinated with the public sector to achieve missions. This is a challenging task because the state or government cannot be embedded in private sector production services.

In her view, all the state needs to do is to use its capabilities and competencies to set missions for addressing societal challenges, including the environment, poverty, and inequality. However, what Mazzucato and other innovation theorists often don't seem to realise is that the capitalist state has always had great deal of involvement in creating those challenges in the first place, through unjust innovation. Historically speaking, capitalism has never operated behind the back of the state. Therefore, the latter would have to be thought as part of the former (hence the term 'capitalist state'). This implies that the state has never been external to the innovation process as a simple regulator or facilitator. Instead, the state has been part of the innovation process through the social division of labour that is in the core of novel technological products and services. This also implies that the capitalist state has never been founded upon any notion of common good. In her latest writings, Mazzucato puts forward the argument that there is a 'common agenda' for the state to promote through missions. Drawing on communitarian critiques of liberalism, she defines the common good in terms of common interests and mutual concerns (Mazzucato, 2023). Yet, historically speaking, there has been conflict of different interests depending on each individual's position in the capitalist division of labour. From this it follows that getting the state to shape the capitalist market and innovation for the sake of common good is a contradiction in terms.

In contrast to Mazzucato and other contemporary theorists' rather uncritical approach to the state, Poulantzas' theory can provide the lenses to view the state in relational terms (just like capital) and therefore to shift research focus on oppressive and exploitative relations and structures which enable innovative technologies. Such a shift, by definition, must take account of the power that is not reducible to the state. In Poulantzas' theory, power is feature of class practices and not of political structures such as the state. In this sense, power is also rooted in the social division of labour and in exploitation. Thus, for example, the division between intellectual and manual labour defines power relations between: those who own knowledge and those who don't; those who sell their manual power (even though manual labour also requires some forms of knowledge) and those who buy it in the market. In the current (neo-liberal) capitalist state, the social division of labour is reflected in skilled-biased technological change. According to Planes-Satorra and Paunov (2017: 7):

> opportunities arise for those having adequate capacities to participate in innovation, as new jobs require their skills and new entrepreneurial opportunities are emerging. Prospects for many others worsen: routine middle-skilled tasks are increasingly being automated, while jobs at the lower end of the distribution are seeing increased demand but are associated with low wages and low levels of job security.

In Poulantzas theory, the state engages in intellectual labour. In this sense it subordinates working classes and actors which tend to engage in manual labour. These include women, immigrants, ethnic minorities, and residents in deprived areas. As he argues:

> In all its apparatuses (that is not only in its ideological apparatuses but also in the repressive and economic ones) the state incarnates intellectual labour as separated from manual labour; this becomes evident provided that the two are not conceived according to a naturalist-positivist distinction. And it is within the capitalist state that the organic relationship between intellectual labour and political domination, knowledge and power is realised in the most consummate manner.
>
> (Poulantzas, 1978: 55–56)

For Poulantzas, given that the state is not an actor, but a relation characterised by internal conflicts and biases, there is a need for coherent project that can be built on this organic relationship and enable the state to act as a unified political force. In the context of contemporary capitalism, the project of science, technology and innovation satisfies this need for coherence and unity. Such a project justifies and unifies different social forces under the institutional umbrella of the capitalist state. This is precisely the reason why innovation can be seen as a dominant discourse and criterion for policy within the capitalist state. According to Jimenezes et al (2025: 1)

> The rise of innovation as a dominant discourse for socioeconomic progress that influences economic and social policy, has been embraced by key societal institutions including education, finance and healthcare, and is widely supported by politicians, policymakers, donors, philanthropists, journalists and academics. This 'innovation turn' has also greatly influenced development policy and practice.

To put it another way, the project of science, technology and innovation brings together competing and conflicting forces, enabling the state to come across as a unified entity.

However, science, technology, and innovation are by no means dominant functions of the state (throughout the different stages of capitalist system). In Poulantzas' theory, the very notion of periodisation of capitalism applies at the level of social formation and not at the level of tendencies of the mode of production (Poulantzas, 1975). Any social formation is highly complex and cannot be necessarily reduced to the consequences of tendencies of the mode of production. Developments in the economic base don't necessarily directly determine the institutional superstructure. Social formations should be reconceptualised in terms of economic, political, and ideological structures. Each of these structures has its own autonomy and it's not the case that the economic structure is always dominant in determining social formations. Poulantzas, following Althusser, distinguishes between determination and dominance. In this theory, the economic structure is not always dominant, albeit determinant. This has implications for the periodisation of capitalism. For example, in feudal stage, it is the political structure that dominates social formations. By contrast, in laissez-faire and monopoly stages, it is the economic structure that both determines and dominates social formations. In state monopoly capitalism it is the state that dominates.

In any case, if one accepts Poulantzas' theory that only social formations can be periodised, one can argue that contemporary capitalism and its state can be clearly distinguished from, say, laissez-faire, monopoly, and state monopoly capitalism. This is because contemporary capitalism and its state are more socially formed through science, technology, and innovation than any other stage of capitalism and its state. In contemporary capitalism, the dominant social mechanisms for controlling production and promoting development are science, technology, and innovation. The state is there to intervene for the sake of reproducing capitalist social relations (Fine and Harris, 1979). In this sense, in contemporary capitalism, the state can be characterised as innovation state without implying that innovation is prioritised as determinant function of the state. Rather, innovation is within an ensemble of distinctive economic, political, and ideological (structural) functions which maintain social cohesion in class-divided societies. From this it follows that the contemporary normal form of state is related to the intensification of political crisis rather than to economic crises tendencies.

Science, technology, and innovation require intellectual labour. The latter is very much supported by the capitalist state through investments in R&D which lead to technological progress and strengthen scientific advantage. The market often fails to generate private funds for R&D investments due to lack of incentives and the high risk of new technologies. The capitalist state, on the other hand, has specific expectations regarding scientific outputs: these are required to serve the interests of free market economy and maintain the process of capital accumulation. Although the capitalist state invests public money in the scientific and technological process of knowledge generation, the benefits of this collective effort tend to be privatised through formally articulated ownership relations, e.g., Intellectual Property Rights (IPRs) for the sake of specific power blocs of classes which maintain their privileged power over technological innovation. Thus, as has been argued by many scholars (Papaioannou, 2018; Foster and Heeks, 2013; Srinivas, 2014; Cozzens and Sutz, 2012), technological innovation world-wide remains exclusive, failing to meet the pressing needs of working classes and the very poor. Due to social division of labour, the needs of working classes and the needs of the very poor are never taken fully on board in R&D of some high-tech innovations, e.g., AI, gene editing, gene drives, etc. Some other high-tech innovations, e.g., information and communication technologies (ICTs), automobiles, etc., have to be modified in order to meet the needs of working classes and the very poor. In fact, all R&D driven innovations embody the properties of social division of labour in their design and development. This means blocs of dominant class privileges and hierarchies are built into their narratives (Winner, 1989).

To make things worse, the assumption that all R&D driven innovations are eventually forces for good and somehow developmental benefits will trickle down to the socially excluded individuals and groups is flawed. R&D driven innovation can be both hierarchical and

> lead to destructive creation, benefiting the few at the expense of the many, leading to low quality jobs, and creating more problems than it solves. Many technologies are deeply implicated in a set of persistent environmental problems. They contribute to the current resource-intensive wasteful and fossil fuel paradigm of mass production and mass consumption.
>
> (Schot and Steinmueller, 2016: 16)

Contemporary innovation theorists have proposed that some of these issues could be addressed through more responsible research and innovation (RRI). However, RRI presupposes that everyone's interests in innovation are taken on board and there are no social divisions in the process of knowledge generation and exploitation. But is this possible within capitalism?

In fact, within capitalism, as Mazzucato (2014) put it, the critical point is to understand the relation between those who bear the risk and contribute public funds to innovation (through the state) and those who appropriate rewards and capital from innovation through the market. But such an understanding presupposes a clear view of the capitalist state as an apparatus that sustains the social division of labour and strives to reproduce it by privatising the collective efforts for innovation and value creation. Although Mazzucato (2018) has criticised the privatisation of innovation and the individualisation of value creation within capitalism, she seems to overlook the historical fact that it is the capitalist state playing the key role in organising such unequal social relations and related power blocs. According to Poulantzas (1978: 59):

> The state redraws and reproduces the social division of labour within its own being: it is thus the carbon-copy of the relations between power and knowledge such as they are reproduced within intellectual labour itself. This process takes place in a range stretching from hierarchical centralised and disciplinary relations to those concentrated in the various layers and nodal-points of decision making and execution.

This Poulantzian understanding of the state leaves no doubt that despite abstract differentiations between its apparatus and the economy or its relative autonomy from dominant classes which secure hegemony, the state is very much interwoven with capitalism. Accumulation of capital through the social division of labour that delivers unjust innovation (i.e. innovations generated in an exploitative context of private ownership) is the primary objective of the capitalist state.

If my understanding so far is correct, then it begs the question of whether the capitalist state can be transformed to prevent appropriation of innovation and development rewards and extraction of public value by power blocs of dominant classes. Can a transformed capitalist state provide directions towards technological innovations which promote social justice? Some Innovation theorists (Mazzucato, 2021, 2014; Block, 2018; Kaplinsky, 2021; Perez, 2016) are optimistic about such state transformation from the top-down with the assistance of new technologies, e.g., ICTs, green technologies, etc. Thus, they envisage a missionary state that can focus its policies on problem-specific challenges and can have the ability to co-ordinate, finance, and direct innovation towards high-value activities for the common good. For innovation historians such as Schot and Steinmueller (2016), this is the equivalent to a 'deep transition' towards system wide transformations. Such transformations can be translated into public missions. For example, to address the challenge of private appropriation of publicly funded innovations, Mazzucato (2014: 189) suggests the following mission:

> Where an applied technological breakthrough is directly financed by the government, the government should in return be able to extract royalty from its application. Returns from royalties earned across sectors and technologies, should be paid into a 'national fund' which the government can use to fund future innovations.

This mission considers the power and willingness of the state to extract royalty from the application of technological innovation as if it was something straightforward. In fact, it is not. The capitalist state might never insist on innovation royalties earned across sectors and technologies for two reasons: first, there is a risk of compromising legitimacy (Papaioannou, 2021) given that different forms of capitalist state (e.g. authoritarian, liberal, welfare, neo-liberal or libertarian forms of state) face different legitimacy constraints; second, the relative autonomy of the capitalist state stops where the slowing down of capital accumulation begins to undermine the structures of the economic system. The latter represent the materiality of all state institutions which tend to be imposed on society.

As I have argued elsewhere (Papaioannou, 2021), we should not expect any radical reconstruction of society and economy to be initiated and/or organised by the capitalist state (the form of which can be more or less entrepreneurial, more or less developmental, depending on its legitimacy constraints). Indeed, the historical lesson that we have learned since the first Industrial Revolution is that capitalism as such cannot change from the top-down let alone be remade by the capitalist state (that strives to reproduce the unjust division of labour in society). Although the periodisation of capitalism implies different social formations throughout the 19th, the 20th, and the 21st centuries, the core of capitalist mode of production remains the same. Evolution within capitalism predominantly concerns the means of production thanks to technological innovation and not the relations of production. Thus, at politics level, what can be remade are some capitalist state policies which stand a chance to challenge free market thinking of neo-liberals and to mitigate the consequences of the free competition. However, such policies would not challenge and/or reshape the core of capitalist mode of production and the exploitative relations which characterise the social division of labour.

It might be speculated that contemporary innovation and development theorists have either 'bought' the argument that 'there is no alternative' to capitalism from the bottom up or they think the radical anti-capitalist argument is an excuse for doing nothing to address the current societal challenges, e.g., poverty, inequality, environment, etc. Whatever the truth is, contemporary innovation and development theorists seem to have given up on radical systemic change from the bottom-up. Instead, they seem to have endorsed short-term missions from the top-down. These missions can potentially unify different fractions of subordinated classes and social forces, maintaining the hegemony of dominant power bloc and legitimising a certain kind of capitalism as socially just. Contemporary innovation theorists don't seem to be concerned much about the fact that capitalism will be reproduced through such missions and unity of illusory interests. The purpose of capital will remain to accumulate profits generated through exploitation, and the purpose of the capitalist state (even though relatively autonomous) will remain to provide a political forum for the capital to justify and legitimise its exploitative relations. To put it another way, systemic change that is in the interest of social equality and environmental sustainability will not be achieved through top-down innovation policies no matter how progressive these might be in terms of promoting social experimentation.

Contemporary innovation and development theorists such as Mazzucato (2021) and Perez (2016) are right of course to argue that 'We are now in a crucial moment in history similar to the 1930s, requiring thinking and measures as bold as those of Keynes, Roosevelt and Beveridge as ambitious as the Bretton Woods agreements' (Perez, 2016: 199). However, such measures will not change the nature of social division of labour but simply adjust capitalism into the new reality of challenges to save it from its own fate of collapse. Would a combination of Keynesian and Schumpeterian innovation state matter? If so for whom? I will try to address these questions in the next section.

6.2 The Role of the State in Innovation

As has been already stressed in Chapter 5, contemporary innovation and development theorists tend to promote a combination of the Keynesian and the Schumpeterian accounts of innovation state as a solution to the problem of directionality of new technologies. This way, what Schot and Steinmueller (2016) have framed as 'transformative change' will become a reality for socio-technical systems which will be directed to address social and environmental challenges.

However, as has been already implied, the combined Keynesian-Schumpeterian innovation and development state tends to rely on the same division of labour that other accounts of capitalist state rely (e.g. neo-classical, Hayekian, etc.). This means that its mission to solve the problems we face today will not go far enough to change the social division of labour and thereby eliminate exploitative relations of private ownership, domination, and oppression within innovative production of goods and services (e.g. IPRs). In this sense, a combined Keynesian-Schumpeterian innovation state does not really matter for social justice. Privatisation of knowledge and appropriation of innovation rewards and extraction of value from power blocs of dominant classes will continue under such capitalist innovation state albeit mitigated by some social welfare policies. This is exactly what happened after the World War II through the social redistributive policies of the welfare state in Europe. Such policies mitigated social inequality but never dared to eliminate it by putting a brake into accumulation of capital by dominant classes. On the contrary, as Claus Offe (1984) shows, the expansion of the post-World War II welfare state promoted the goal of capital accumulation. This goal clearly contradicts the goal of social welfare provision. For Offe, this contradiction is irresolvable. Therefore, welfare states tend to generate more policy failures and conflicts than they resolve.

It might be argued that what really matters for social justice is to build an innovation state the role of which is not to redraw and/or reproduce the capitalist social division of labour. Such a non-capitalist and transformative state will reconcile intellectual and manual labour and will eliminate private ownership of knowledge and exploitative relations of innovative production. However, all these prospects are theoretical. The key set of questions that we should be asking is rather practical. Namely, is a non-capitalist innovation state feasible in the 21st century? If so, does a non-capitalist innovation state have to be necessarily a socialist one in the Poulantzian sense of the term (i.e. democratic socialism)? Is there a pluralism of new alternatives from the bottom up, including some going beyond Poulantzas' democratic socialism (i.e. his theory of the democratic socialist state)?

Let me attempt to answer these questions by stating the following: Poulantzas' theory is crucial for understanding the state as a social relation that reflects the exploitative and oppressive division of labour within society. This understanding is missing from contemporary innovation theories of the entrepreneurial state, leading them to reach superficial conclusions about changing capitalism from the top-down. However, despite its importance for the innovation state, Poulantzas' theory also faces limitations. First, as many scholars (Bruff, 2012; Mueller, 2019) have pointed out, it remains structuralist Marxist and unable to account fully for the importance of agency in social change. Second, this theory remains somewhat abstract and unable to fully account for empirical developments towards multiple alternatives to the capitalist state of innovation. With exception his *Fascism and Democracy* (1974) (that applies the conceptual and epistemological formulations of his *Political Power and Social Classes*, 1973), Poulantzas maintains a rather formalistic approach to theorising the interplay between state, institutions, and political struggles. This implies difficulty of grasping the plurality and the role of social movements and campaigns which are not rooted in class struggle. For Poulantzas, political mobilisation to transform state structures and to alter policies can only be explained in terms of class struggle. Movements and campaigns which are not directly rooted in class struggle seem to be less effective in challenging and capturing the state. Often these movements and campaigns are not viewed as genuine alliances.

In Poulantzas's theory, as Jessop (1982: 165) argues,

> state power … corresponds unequivocally to the interests of the power bloc and … the working class cannot advance its fundamental interests … and/or secure its own hegemony through the capitalist state … . Yet, while the dominated classes cannot establish their own state power simply through the capture of the existing state apparatus and must develop their own class unity in and through the struggle for a new form of state, they are present in the capitalist state in a disunified, fragmented manner and can advance their particular isolated 'economic-corporate' interests

> through this state to the extent that such advances also sustain bourgeois hegemony.

Poulantzas' emphasis on the importance of working classes unity takes us back to Gramsci who understood the capitalist state to play crucial role in reconciling particular interests of different fractions within working classes through projects and hegemonic visions in an 'illusionary' notion of general interest (Jessop, 2016: 215). However, this seems to underplay the importance of radical yet fragmented movements and campaigns in challenging the capitalist state and offering alternatives. As Jackson and Lamb (2021: 6) point out, such movements and campaigns are part of civil society and range from

> concerned consumer shopping for fair trade goods in the supermarket, the car-free families showing how we can cut carbon emissions, volunteers helping settle refugees, and people protesting against local fracking, to entire grassroots movements of huge NGOs whose operations span the globe.

Given the continuous crises of contemporary capitalism and the inability of this system of political economy to address developmental challenges such as climate change and deep socio-economic inequalities, various such movements world-wide point towards public actions and campaigns which aim at changing the social division of labour and promoting transition to an innovation and development state that takes on board the interests of everyone (i.e. innovators, regulators and publics). Indeed, so much social and political change has come about not because of 'statolatry' (Gramsci, 1975) but because of civil society that has imagined and felt the responsibility to act for better world (Jackson and Lamb, 2021). Quite often, public actions and campaigns are bottom-up mobilisations against innovation injustice (Papaioannou, 2018). They are motivated by what Young (2011) calls 'personal responsibility' for justice in innovation systems and related structures. According to her 'what it means to be responsible is for a person to maintain control over his or her actions and their consequences and to make sure that they and only bear their costs' (Young, 2011: 23). The radical direction of innovation and development can only change from the bottom-up when individuals realise that the capitalist division of labour fails to deliver innovations and values for everyone and thereby feel responsible for taking political action (Arvidsson, 2020). This bottom-up change is by definition conflictual. Political action aims to undermine the coherence of capitalist state apparatus and thereby prevent it from reproducing the social division of labour. As Glasius and Ishkanian (2015) point out, such action takes place at certain points in time when dissatisfaction with the capitalist state and the free market is very high. Responsible public activists see a window of opportunity for change of social relations and technological paradigms.

The capitalist innovation and development state, especially during the historical dominance of neo-liberalism, has justified exclusion on the grounds of individual freedom to maximise exchange-value of innovation through unregulated globalising markets. In contrast, a non-capitalist innovation state can justify inclusion on the grounds of collective freedom to maximise use-value of innovation. Given the crisis of neo-liberal globalisation, a non-capitalist innovation state can regain power and impose constraints on global capital's interests in exclusive innovation and development. Instead of exclusive technologies, it can promote innovations from the bottom up that have more use-value than exchange-value and satisfy basic human needs. From India to Peru, there have been numerous bottom-up initiatives for inclusive innovations (either grassroots or frugal) which have use-value simply because they address basic human needs (Kothari, 2021).

6.3 Bottom-Up Initiatives of Innovation and Development

Jackson and Lamb (2021) provide an extensive account of such initiatives which are no longer wishful thinking but rather build up bottom-up alternatives, meeting real human needs. For example, according to them (Jackson and Lamb, 2021: 132):

> Web-based, non-profit initiatives are proliferating, based on citizens sharing and collaborating across borders for the common good – whether creating high-quality open-source software from Linux operating system or Wikipedia's extraordinary 46 million articles in 300 languages accessed by 1.4 billion unique devices every month.

Subverting and appropriating technologies for better alternatives to capitalist innovation and development state and for better futures is what Smith and Fressoli (2021) call post-automation. The latter is, in essence, a bottom-up set of capabilities which open sociotechnical alternatives to capitalist accumulation and the exploitative division of labour. These capabilities are already important for social movements which promote algorithmic justice, data commons, etc. Martell (2023) notes that people around the world already practice alternatives, including innovative digital alternatives such as Mastodon (which has attracted an exodus from Twitter) and democratically owned technologies. Precondition for these alternatives to scale up is institutional change that does not reproduce the exploitative division of labour.

In a recent article, Smith and Stirling (2018: 66–67) also list a number of other innovations:

> Wind energy, community supported agriculture, social technologies, car clubs, free software, open hardware, repair cafes, participatory design, agro-ecology, eco-housing, recycling, shared machine shops rainwater harvesting, complementary currencies, credit unions, socially useful production, seed swapping, community energy cooperatives, garden sharing, community forestry, green spaces and many, many other ideas and practices for sustainable development began in innovative grassroots activity.

The common denominator of all these initiatives seems to be the absence of a social division between intellectual and manual labour. As a result of it, there are no hierarchical relations of domination and oppression in the process of generation and application of new knowledge. Instead, there is a new commons generated in the form of 'general intellect' (Arvidsson, 2020: 25). According to Smith and Stirling (2018: 69):

> People bring different forms of expertise and experience into collective behaviour. It can be technical knowledge built up through one's job or professional training, such as accounting and doing books for the initiative or some engineering knowledge. Or it can be vital expert knowledge dynamics in the neighbourhood and using one standing or contacts to bring people on board and earn legitimacy.

Absence of hierarchical relations creates the potential for more democratic innovation and development state that can politically direct technologies and services towards social justice. It is worth pointing out here that a non-capitalist innovation and development state is not necessarily a socialist state. This is not because a socialist state cannot be innovative or developmental but because democratic socialism can be considered to be just one alternative to capitalism. Although this alternative has been theorised in both the global North and global South through the Marxian and neo-Marxist critiques of the capitalist political economy as a transitional stage towards the teleology of a classless society, attempts for its implementation have been problematical in several respects (e.g. democratic engagement) and historically inconsistent with the theory. In the 21st century there may be a plurality of alternatives (including democratic socialist, pluralist socialist, post-socialist, post-colonial, and post-development ones) emerging through public action and social movements especially in the global South. Innovation and development theory should explore this plurality of alternatives further to guide innovation and development practice. It should, for example, explore whether a non-capitalist innovation state might not have to focus on economic growth or to organise centrally knowledge and production activities for the purpose of just innovation. In addition, a non-capitalist innovation state might be guided by human rights and therefore be able to politically direct innovation towards satisfying needs of equal members of society.

It might be argued that a non-capitalist innovation and development state that is democratic might in theory be even more appropriate for promoting a conception of equality in terms of the relations between individuals in society than a democratic socialist state. Comparing to the latter that conceives equality in terms of distribution of resources, the former can focus on establishing a society of equals through innovation and development. In the absence of any social division of labour (including racial and gendered forms), this implies reduction of hierarchy, oppression, discrimination, domination and so forth through innovations such as ICTs (e.g. by recording live cases of oppression and discrimination and addressing them immediately) and new life sciences (e.g. by reducing genetic disorders). A non-capitalist innovation and development state might even be more pragmatic than a socialist innovation and development state in the sense that the former's approach to justice is driven by inequalities on the ground whereas the latter's approach is driven by an ideal theory of principles which would create a society of equals. A more pragmatic non-capitalist innovation and development state also implies the acceptance that not all relational inequalities will be eliminated. There may be non-capitalist forms of oppression e.g., patriarchy deeply embedded in culture, religion, and history of some societies. A non-ideal theory of relational justice should carefully study and understand the nature of such forms of oppression in order to find ways towards just outcomes.

Finally, it can be also proposed that a non-capitalist innovation and development state can even allow many different 'societies of equals' at the same time, depending on what kind of precise relations people accept as justified in their societies. As Wolff (2015: 15) put it, what these societies

> have in common is that they avoid various objectionable social relations. These objectionable social relations will fall into at least two groups. One picks out a range of asymmetrical relations, as set out above (oppression, exploitation, etc) and hence identifies various forms of inequality. The other concerns relations of alienation or estrangement. This latter group picks out the idea that a society of equals is, after all, a *society*, and therefore, should have a certain fabric of mutual connectedness.

In theory, a vision of non-capitalist innovation and development state can politically direct new technologies to identify and remedy both groups of objectionable social relations. In this sense, it can enable holistic change towards a democratic society of equals.

6.4 Conclusion

This chapter has sought to address the question of what kind of innovation and development state matters for social justice. It has done so by revisiting Poulantzas' theory of the state and going beyond it to consider alternatives to capitalist innovation and development state from the bottom up. Contemporary theorists of the state of innovation and development have not paid attention to the ideas of Poulantzas. This lacuna in scholarly attention has implications for failing to understand the state of innovation and development as a social relation that reflects the capitalist division of labour. The argument put forward in this chapter has been that theorists of innovation and development should learn from Poulantzas and should re-think the state not in terms of combining Keynesian and Schumpeterian accounts but in terms of changing the fundamental division of labour within capitalism. It is this social division that underpins the state and diverts the direction of innovation towards exploitation and injustice. Unless it is changed or eliminated from the bottom up and through public action of politically responsible individuals, the social division of labour within capitalism will carry on producing exclusions from innovation and development, promoting private ownership of dominant social classes of technologies. This chapter has discussed the possibility of a non-capitalist innovation and development state, recognising the shortcomings of Poulantzas' theory. These shortcomings have to do with the formalistic and structuralist nature of this theory that does not fully account for the plurality of bottom-up alternatives to the capitalist state. Yet such alternatives can only be the fruit of public action and campaigning for closing social divisions in innovative production. Instead of these divisions, a non-capitalist innovation state can focus on knowledge sharing for products and processes which have use-value. It can do so by restricting or even eliminating IPR regimes and promoting collective action.

Note

1 The notion of market fundamentalism has been used by scholars such as Block (2013) to describe the 1980s' neo-liberal turn to free market competition and limited government. These institutions have been presented as natural, overlooking the importance of legal and institutional practices which very much shape them. For example, as Davis and Klare (2010: 409) remind us '... the so-called "freedom of contract" consists of negotiation conducted and agreement made within governmentally structured framework of mutual pressure and coercion'.

Conclusion

This small book has integrated old and new work of mine in explaining why justice in innovation and development matters. Although not the same, innovation and development are interrelated processes. Both of them are concerned with change that impacts on individuals, their societies, and the environment. The book has sought to apply non-ideal political theory in addressing questions of justice in innovation and development from a relational perspective. It has argued that innovative technologies which impact on development presuppose that requirements of relational justice can be met in order for them to be accepted and legitimised as a positive force of change in society. The idea of relational justice derives from the critique of distributive theories, including egalitarian liberal and utilitarian perspectives, which emphasise the primacy of material resources as a currency of justice. In fact, material resources or material factors are far from being the only concerns of an egalitarian theory of justice. By contrast, relational theories, including justice as equal respect, recognition and participation, and capability and ubuntu emphasise the primacy of relations in society. The main concern of relational justice is to create a society of equals. In this sense, it also applies in innovation and development. To what extent a society of equals can be both innovative and developmental? How can innovators, regulators, and publics act in terms of relations of equality and not in terms of relations of domination and oppression?

To answer these questions, this book built on three principles: equity, participation, and recognition. These principles, which were introduced and theorised in previous writings, constitute the foundations of a theory of relational justice in innovation and development. This book

DOI: 10.4324/9781003652083-8

has suggested that only non-ideal principles of equity, participation, and recognition can embody solutions to empirical problems of unequal generation and diffusion of emerging technologies. The normative direction of innovation systems and developmental projects in the 21st century very much depends on relational principles generated from the bottom-up. Radical change of social relations of power at different scales can only come through public action and campaigning for justice in innovation and development. The relational idea of justice in innovation and development is predominantly political because it focuses on social relations of the generation and diffusion of new knowledge and emerging technologies. It therefore presents inclusion not simply as an abstract ideal but as a concrete and relational historical condition framed in non-ideal terms of justice. This is an approach that ideal theories of justice fail to grasp due to their lack of empirical foundations that leads to persistent idealism. Therefore, such theories should not be applied to govern emerging technologies and developmental projects on the ground. Justice in artificial intelligence (AI) and machine learning (ML) technologies, for example, has more to do with how they enable equal respect, recognition, and participation of certain marginalised and excluded social groups and less to do with how they are equally distributed to these groups. Equal distribution of AI and ML technologies is a secondary concern for the relational theory of justice in innovation. This means that equal distribution is required only if there is concrete evidence that it will lead to equalising relations between innovators, regulators, and publics.

Ideal theories consider the state to be the main political institution in charge of implementing principles of social justice for the sake of an abstract common good. The latter is rarely defined or analysed in detail. In fact, it is a non-historical notion or a theoretical construction that has limited political implications within capitalism. Yet this book has argued that the state is vulnerable to competing economic interests and power blocks which do not necessarily promote justice in innovation and development. Instead of top-down state politics, bottom-up grassroots movements and campaigns for relational justice in innovation and development can implement relational principles of justice. In arguing so, I don't consider the state to be redundant in the debate about justice in innovation and development. Rather, I consider the state to be one political force that plays a role in implementing bottom-up principles of justice in innovation and development. The other political forces are grassroots activists and campaigners who need to work closely with a progressive political state to deliver just outcomes of innovation and development. Activist participation in political processes of the state can have positive impact on justice in innovation and development.

However, this is not to say that it has always been the case. Historically, we have also witnessed some activist participation in politics, having negative impact on justice in innovation, e.g., Genetically Modified Organisms (GMOs), and development, e.g., late industrialisation. The state is not of course a unified actor as some contemporary innovation and development theorists argue. Instead, it can be seen from a Poulantzian perspective as the material condensation of relationships between social classes and class fractions, including innovators, regulators, and publics. The state's relative autonomy consists of its capacity to often ignore demands not only from activists but also from powerful interest groups, and instead focus on public policies for the sake of its own legitimacy. Yet, the state can face legitimacy crisis if it pushes for a direction of innovation and development that is not consistent with its political nature or is not justified to civil society.

Bibliography

Adewale, A. R. (2017) 'Import Substitution Industrialisation and Economic Growth – Evidence from the Group of BRICS Countries' *Future Business Journal,* Vol.3, pp.138–158.

Alden, E. and Litan, R. E. (2017) 'A New Deal for the Twenty-First Century' *Council on Foreign Relations*, Available at: www.cfr.org/sites/default/files/report_pdf/Renewing_America_Twenty_First_Century_Deal_OR.pdf

Amin, S. (1990) *Delinking: Towards a Polycentric World*, London: Zed Books.

Amsden, A. (1989) *Asia's Next Giant: South Korea and Late Industrialisation*, New York and Oxford: Oxford University Press.

Anderson, E. S. (1999) 'What Is the Point of Equality?' *Ethics*, Vol.109, No.2, pp.287–337.

Anderson, E. S. (2010) *The Imperative of Integration*, Princeton, NJ: Princeton University Press.

Arneson, R. (2004) 'Luck Egalitarianism: Interpreted and Defended' *Philosophical Topics,* Vol.32, pp.1–20.

Arun, C. (2020) 'AI and Global South: Designing for Other Worlds' in M. D. Dubber (ed) *The Oxford Handbook of Ethics of AI*, Oxford: Oxford Handbooks Online, Available at: https://global.oup.com/academic/product/the-oxford-handbook-of-ethics-of-ai-9780190067397

Arvidsson, A. (2020) 'Capitalism and the Commons' *Theory, Culture and Society*, Vol.37, No.2, pp.3–30.

Baran, P. (1957) *The Political Economy of Growth*, New York: Monthly Review Press.

Barry B. (1995) *Justice as Impartiality: A Treatise on Social Justice*, Edition II, Oxford: Oxford University Press.

Barry, B. (2005) *Why Social Justice Matters*, Cambridge: Polity Press.

Bentham, J. (1970) 'An Introduction to the Principles of Morals and Legislation' in J. H. Burns and H. L. Hart (eds) *The Collected Works of Jeremy Bentham*, Oxford: Clarendon Press.

Berlin, I. (1975) 'Two Concepts of Liberty' in D. Miller (ed) *Liberty*, Oxford: Oxford University Press.

Binns, R. (2018) 'Fairness in Machine Learning: Lessons from Political Philosophy' *Proceedings of Machine Learning Research*, Vol.81, pp.1–11.

Block, F. (1987) 'Beyond Relative Autonomy: State Managers as Historical Subjects' in F. Block (ed) *Revising State Theory: Essays in Politics and Post-industrialism*, Philadelphia: Temple University Press.

Block, F. (2008) 'Swimming Against the Current: The Rise of a Hidden Developmental State in the United States' *Politics and Society*, Vol.36, No.2, pp.169–206.

Block, F. (2011) 'Innovation and the Invisible Hand of Government' in F. Block and R. M. Keller (eds) *State of Innovation: The US Government's Role in Technology Development*, Boulder and London: Paradigm Publishers.

Block, F. (2013) 'Relational Work and Law: Recapturing the Legal Realist Critique of Market Fundamentalism' *Journal of Law and Society*, Vol.40, No.1, pp.27–48.

Block, F. (2018) *Capitalism: The Future of an Illusion*, Oakland: University of California Press.

Block, F. and Keller, M. (2011) *State of Innovation: The US Government's Role in Technology Development*, London: Paradigm Publishers.

Brett, E. A. (2009) *Reconstructing Development Theory*, Basingstoke: Palgrave Macmillan.

Bruff, I. (2012) 'The Relevance of Nicos Poulantzas for Contemporary Debates on the International' *International Politics*, Vol.49, No.2, pp.113–129.

Buchanan, A., Cole, T. and Keohane, R. O. (2011) 'Justice in the Diffusion of Innovation' *Journal of Political Philosophy*, Vol.19, No.3, pp.306–332.

Burlamaqui, L. (2012) 'Knowledge Governance: An Analytical Perspective and its Policy Implications' in L. Burlamaqui, A. Castro and R. Kattel (eds) *Knowledge Governance: Reasserting the Public Interest*, London: Anthem Press.

Bush, V. (1945) *Science, the Endless Frontier*, 2nd Edition, Washington DC: US Office of Scientific Research and Development.

Caldas, J. C., Costa, A. N. and Burns, T. R. (2006) 'Rethinking Economics: The Potential Contribution of the Classics' *Cambridge Journal of Economics*, Vol.31, No.1, pp.25–40.

Callinicos, A. T. (2000) *Equality*, Cambridge: Polity.

Carter, A. (2020) 'The Moral Dimension of AI-Assisted Decision-Making: Some Practical Perspectives from Front Lines' *Daedalus: The Journal of the American Academy of Arts and Sciences*, Vo.151, No.2, pp.299–308.

Chambers, R. (2017) *Can We Know Better? Reflections for Development*, Rugby: Practical Action Publishing.

Chandler, D. (2023) *Free and Equal: What Would a Fair Society Look Like?* London: Allen Lane.

Charles, K. and Williams, D. (2001) 'What Do We Know about Economic Growth? Or Why Don't We Know Very Much?' *World Development*, Vol.29, No.1, pp.1–22.

Choi, J., Dutz, M. A. and Usman, Z. (eds) (2020) *The Future of Work in Africa: Harnessing the Potential of Digital Technologies for All*, Washington, D.C., World Bank Publications.

Coeckelbergh. M. (2022) 'Forward' in D. Okaibedi Eke, K. Wakunuma and S. Akintoye (eds) *Responsible AI in Africa*, Leicester: Palgrave Macmillan, Available at: https://link.springer.com/book/10.1007/978-3-031-08215-3

Cohen, G. A. (1989) 'On the Currency of Egalitarian Justice' *Ethics,* Vol.99, pp.906–944.

Cohen, G. A. (2008) *Rescuing Justice and Equality*, Cambridge, Massachusetts: Harvard University Press.

Cohen, G. A. and Graham, K. (1990) 'Self-Ownership, Communism and Equality' *Proceedings of the Aristotelian Society*, Vol.64, pp.25–61.

Collington, R. and Mazzucato, M. (2022) 'Beyond Outsourcing: Re-embedding the State in Public Value Production' IIPP Working Paper 14, pp.1–38, Available at: www.ucl.ac.uk/bartlett/public-purpose/publications/2022/aug/beyond-outsourcing-re-embedding-state-public-value-production

Constantinescu, M., Vica, C. and Voinea, C. (2022) 'Blame it on the AI? On the Moral Responsibility of Artificial Moral Advisors' *Philosophy and Technology*, Vol.35, No.35, pp.1–16.

Coutinho, C. N. (2012) *Gramsci's Political Thought*, Leiden and Boston: Brill.

Cozzens, S. and Sutz, J. (2012) *Innovation in Informal Settings: A Research Agenda*, Ottawa: IDRC.

Davidson, S. and Potts, J. (2022) '*The Entrepreneurial State and the Platform Economy*' in C. Wennberg and C. Sandström (eds) *Questioning the Entrepreneurial State: Status-Quo, Pitfalls and the Need for Credible Innovation Policy*, Cham: Springer.

Davis, D. and Klare, K (2010) 'Transformative Constitutionalism and the Common and Customary Law' *South African Journal on Human Rights*, Vol.26, No.3, pp.403–509.

DeGraaff, S. Wanzenbock, I. and Frenken, K. (2025) 'The Politics of Directionality in Innovation Policy through the Lens of Policy Process Frameworks' *Science and Public Policy*, Vol.52, pp.418–432.

Dignum, V. (2022) 'Relational Artificial Intelligence' Available at: https://arxiv.org/abs/2202.07446

Dryzek, J. S. and Dunleavy, P. (2009) *Theories of Democratic State*, Basingstoke: Palgrave Macmillan.

Dworkin, R. (1977) *Taking Rights Seriously*, London: Duckworth.

Dworkin, R. (1981) 'What Is Equality? II Equality of Resources' *Philosophy and Public Affairs,* Vol.10, pp.283–345.

Dworkin, R. (2000) *Sovereign Virtue: The Theory and Practice of Equality*, Cambridge MA: Harvard University Press.

Eisenstadt, S. (1966) *Modernisation: Protest and Change*, Englewood Cliffs, NJ: Prentice-Hall.

Escobar, A. (1995) *Encountering Development: The Making and Unmaking of the Third World*, Princeton and Oxford: Princeton University Press.

Escobar, A. (2019) 'Dudley Seers (1929–1983)' in D. Simon (ed) *Key Thinkers on Development*, London and New York: Routledge.

Esteva, G. (1992) 'Development' in W. Sachs (ed) *The Development Dictionary: A Guide to Knowledge as Power*, London: Zed Books, pp.6–25.

Eubanks, V. (2018) *Automating Inequality: How High-Tech Tools Profile, Police, and Punish the Poor*, New York: St. Martin's Press.

Fagerberg, J., Martin, B. and Sloth Andersen, E. (2013) *Innovation Studies: Evolution and Future Challenges*, Oxford: Oxford University Press.

Feenberg, A. (1991) *Critical Theory of Technology*, New York and Oxford: Oxford.

Ferguson, J. (1990) *The Anti-politics Machine: Development Depoliticisation and Bureaucratic Power in Lesoto*, Cambridge: Cambridge University Press.

Fine, B. and Harris, L. (1979) *Rereading Capital*, London and Basingstoke: The Macmillan Pres.

Fischer, A. M. (2019) 'Bringing Development Back into Development Studies' *Development and Change*, Vol.50, No.2, pp.426–444.

Fortuny-Sicart, A. and Pansera, M. (2024) 'Giving Digital Delivery Platforms a Different Direction: Coopcycle as a Case Study that Integrates Democratic and Eco-Social Values into Organisational Design and Technology' *The Journal of Responsible Innovation*, Special Issue on 'Critiquing the Direction for Innovation – The Role of Justice and Exnovation'. Vol.11, No.1, pp.1–22.

Foster, C. and Heeks, R. (2013) 'Conceptualising Inclusive Innovation: Modifying Systems of Innovation Framework to Understand Diffusion of New Technology to Low Income Consumers' *European Journal of Development Research*, Vol.25, No.3, pp.333–355.

Fougere, M. and Harding, N. (2012) 'On the Limits of What Can Be Said about 'Innovation': Interplay and Contracts between Academic and Policy Discourses' in K. E. Sveiby, P. Gripenberg, B. Segercrantz (eds) *Challenging the Innovation Paradigm*, London: Routledge, pp.35–58.

Fourie, C., Schuppert, F. and Walliman-Helmner, I. (2015) 'The Nature and Distinctiveness of Social Equality: An Introduction' in C. Fourie, F. Schuppert, and I. Walliman-Helmner (eds) *Social Equality: On What It Means to be Equals*, Oxford: Oxford University Press, pp.1–17.

Foxon, T. and Kanger, L. (2018) 'Social Trends and New Geographies' in IPSP (eds), *Rethinking Society for the 21st Century: Report of the International Panel on Social Progress.* Cambridge: Cambridge University Press, pp.9–40.

Frank, A. G. (1967) *Capitalism and Underdevelopment in Latin America*, New York: Monthly Review Press.

Fraser, N. (2003) 'Social Justice in the Age of Identity Politics: Redistribution, Recognition and Participation' in N. Fraser and A. Honneth (eds) *Redistribution or Recognition? A Political-Philosophical Exchange*, London and New York: Verso, pp.7–109.

Fraser, N. (2008) 'Reframing Justice in a Globalising World' in K. Olson (ed) *Adding Insult to Injury: Nancy Fraser Debates and Her Critiques*, London: Verso, pp.273–291.

Fraser, N. and Honneth, A. (2003) (eds) *Redistribution or Recognition? A Political-Philosophical Exchange*, London and New York: Verso, pp.1–276.

Freeman, C. (1981) (ed) *Technological Innovation and National Economic Performance*, Aalborg: Aalborg University Press.

Freeman, C. (1991) 'Technological Progress and Quality of Life' *Science and Public Policy*, Vol.18, No.6, pp.407–418.

Freeman, C., Oldham, G. H. G., Cooper, C. M., Sinclair, T. C. and Achilladeelis, B. G. (1971) 'The Goals of R&D in the 1970s' *Science Studies*, Vol.1, pp.357–406.

Freeman, C. and Soete, L. (1997) *The Economics of Industrial Innovation*, London: Routledge.

Friedman, M. (2017) 'The Relation between Economic and Political Freedom' in R. Leeson and C. G. Dalm (eds) *Milton Freedman on Freedom: Selections from the Collected Works of Milton Friedman*, Stanford: Hoover Institution Press Publication.

Fuchs, L. and Ziegler, R. (2025) 'Critiquing the Direction for Innovation: The Interplay of Why, How, and What', *Journal of Responsible Innovation*, Vol.12, No.1, p.2549956, DOI 10.1080/23299460.2025.2549956

Fukuyama, F. (1995) *Trust: The School Virtues and the Creation of Prosperity*, Harmondsworth: Penguin.

Gaskell, G. (2004) 'Science Policy and Society: The British Debate over GM Agriculture' *Current Opinion in Biotechnology*, Vol.15, pp.241–245.

Gerschenham, A. (1962) *Economic Backwardness in Historical Perspective: A Book of Essays*, Cambridge MA: Belknap Press of the Harvard University.

Giddens, A. (1984) *The Constitution of Society*, Cambridge: Polity Press.

Gigerenzer, G. and Selten, R. (2001) *Bounded Rationality and Adaptive Toolbox*, Cambridge MA: The MIT Press.

Gill, A. S. and Germann, S. (2022) 'Conceptual and Normative Approaches to AI Governance for a Global Digital Ecosystem Supportive of the UN Sustainable Development' *AI and Ethics*, Vol.2, pp.293–301.

Glasius, M. and Ishkanian, A. (2015) 'Surreptitious Symbiosis: Engagement between Activists and NGOs' *Voluntas: International Journal of Voluntary and Nonprofit Organisations*, Vol.26, No.6, pp.1–36. Available at: https://eprints.lse.ac.uk/60128/1/Glasius_Ishkanian_Surreptitious-symbiosis_2014.pdf

Godin, B. (2008) 'Innovation: The History of a Category' Working Paper, Available at: www.csiic.ca/PDF/IntellectualNo1.pdf

Godin, B. (2020) *The Idea of Technological Innovation: A Brief Alternative History*, Cheltenham: Edward Elgar.

Gramsci, A. (1975) *Prison Notebooks*, New York: Columbia University Press.

Grugel, J., Nem Singh, J., Fontana, L. B. and Uhlin, A. (2017) (eds) *Demanding Justice in The Global South*, Basingstoke and New York: Palgrave Macmillan.

Gyekye, K. (1997) *Tradition and Modernity: Philosophical Reflections on the African Experience*, Oxford: Oxford University Press.

Harriss, J. (2014) 'Development Theories' in B. Currie-Alder, D. M. Malone and R. Medhora (ed) *International Development: Ideas, Experience and Prospects*, Oxford: Oxford University Press.

Harriss, J. (2021) 'Returning to the Great Transformation' in T. Allen and A. Thomas (eds) *Poverty and Development in the 21st Century*, Oxford: Oxford University Press.

Hart, G. (2001) 'Development Critiques in the 1990s: Culs dee Sac and Promising Paths' *Progress in Human Geography*, Vol.25, No.4, pp.649–658.

Harvey, D. (1992) 'Social Justice, Postmodernism and the City' *International Journal of Urban and Regional Research*, Vol.16, No.4, pp.588–601.

Harvey, D. (2005) *A Brief History of Neoliberalism*, Oxford: Oxford University Press.

Hayek, F. A. (1944) *The Road to Serfdom*, London: Routledge.

Hayek, F. A. (1948) *Individualism and Economic Order*, South Bend Indiana: Gateway Editions, Ltd.

Hayek, F. A. (1960) *The Constitution of Liberty*, London: Routledge and Kegan Paul.

Hayek, F. A. (1967) *Studies in Philosophy, Politics and Economics*, London: Routledge and Kegan Paul.

Hayek, F. A. (1973) *Law, Legislation and Liberty*, Vol.1, London: Routledge and Kegan Paul.

Hayek, F. A. (1982) *Law, Legislation and Liberty: A New Statement of the Liberal Principles of Justice and Political Economy*, London: Routledge and Kegan Paul.

Heeks, R. and Renken, J. (2018) 'Data Justice for Development: What Would It Mean?' *Information Development*, Vol.34, No.1, pp.90–102.

Hettne, B. (2009) *Thinking about Development*, London and New York: Zed Books.

HM Government (2023) *Pro-Innovation Regulation of Technologies Review*, London, Available at: www.gov.uk/government/collections/pro-innovation-regulation-of-technologies-review

Holden, B. (1996) (ed) *The Ethical Dimensions of Global Change*, London: Macmillan.

Horner, R. and Hulme, D. (2019) 'From International to Global Development: New Geographies of 21st Century Development' *Development and Change*, Vol.50, No.2, pp.495–510.

Hoy, C. and Sumner, A. (2020) 'Growth with Adjectives: Global Poverty and Inequality after the Pandemic' Working Paper 537, Centre for Global Development, Available at: www.cgdev.org/publication/growth-adjectives-global-poverty-and-inequality-after-pandemic

IEA-International Energy Agency (2016) *World Energy Outlook 2016*, Paris, France: OECD/IEA.

IPP (2020) *Reshaping Global Health Systems in Response to Covid-19*, UCL IIPP COVID-19 Briefing Papers 03 (June).

Jackson, B. and Lamb, H. (2021) *From Anger to Action*, London and Lanham: Rowman and Littlefield Publishing.

Jacobs, M. and Mazzucato, M. (2016) (eds) *Rethinking Capitalism: Economics and Policy for Sustainable and Inclusive Growth*, Chichester: Blackwell Publishing.

Jessop, B. (1982) *The Capitalist State*, New York: New York University Press.

Jessop, B. (2016) *The State: Past, Present and Future*, Cambridge: Polity Press.

Jimenez, A., Pansera, M. and Abdelnour, S. (2025) 'Imposing Innovation: How 'Innovation Speak' Maintains Postcolonial Exclusion in Peru' *World Development*, Vol.189, pp.1–10.

Jones, K. (2023) *AI Governance and Human Rights: Resetting the Relationship*, London: Chatham House.

Juma, C. (2016) *Innovation and Its Enemies: Why People Resist New Technologies*, Oxford: Oxford University Press.

Kaplinsky, R. (2021) *Sustainable Futures: An Agenda for Action*, Cambridge: Polity.

Kaplinsky, R., Chataway, J., Clark, N., Hanlin, R., Kale, D., Muraguri, L., Papaioannou, T., Robbins, P. and Wamae, W. (2009) 'Below the Radar: What Does Innovation in Emerging Economies Have to Offer Other Low-Income Economies?' *International Journal of Technology Management & Sustainable Development,* Vol.8, No.3, pp.177–197.

Karlson, N., Sandström, C. and Wennberg, K. (2021) 'Bureaucrats or Markets in Innovation Policy? A Critique of the Entrepreneurial State' *Review of Austrian Economics*, Vol.34, pp.81–95.

Keynes, J. M. (1932) *Economic Possibilities for Our Grandchildren' Essays in Persuasion*, New York: Harcourt Brace, pp.358–373.

Keynes, J. M. (1936) *The General Theory of Employment, Interest and Money*, New York: Harcourt Brace.

Keynes, J. M. (2013) 'The End of Laissez-Faire' in M. Keynes, E. Johnson, and D. E. Moggridge (eds)*The Collected Writings of John Maynard Keynes IX Essays in Persuasion*, Cambridge: Cambridge University Press, pp.272–294.

Kothari, A. (2021) 'These Alternative Economies Are Inspirations for a Sustainable World' *The Scientific American*, June, Available at: www.scientificamerican.com/article/these-alternative-economies-are-inspirations-for-a-sustainable-world/

Kothari, U. (ed) (2005) *A Radical History of Development Studies: Individuals, Institutions and Ideologies,* London: Zed Books.

Kymlicka, W. (1990) *Contemporary Political Philosophy: An Introduction*, Oxford: Oxford University Press.

Laclau, E. (1975) 'The Specificity of the Political: Around the Poulantzas-Miliband Debate' *Economy and Society*, Vol.5, No.1, pp.87–110.

Langdon, J. (2013) 'Decolonising Development Studies: Reflections on Critical Pedagogies in Action' *Canadian Journal of Development Studies/ Revue Canadienne d'études du développement*, Vol.34, No.3, pp.384–399.

Li, P., Yang, J., Islam, M. A. and Ren, S. (2023) 'Making AI Less "Thirsty" Uncovering and Addressing the Secrete Water Footprint of AI Models', Available at: https://arxiv.org/abs/2304.03271

Locke, J. (1988) *Two Treatises of Government*, 3rd Edition, Cambridge: Cambridge University Press.

Lyons, D. (1984) 'Utility and Rights' in J. Waldron (ed) *Theories of Rights*, Oxford: Oxford University Press.

Mackintosh, M. (1992) 'Introduction' in M. Wuyts, M. Mackintosh and T. Hewitt (eds) *Development Policy and Public Action*, Oxford: Oxford University Press.

Madianou, M. (2019) 'Technocolonianism: Digital Innovation and Data Practices in the Humanitarian Response to Refugee Crises' *Social Media+ Society*, July–September, Vol.5, No.3, pp.1–13, Available at: https://journals.sagepub.com/doi/pdf/10.1177/2056305119863146

Mantouvalou, V. and Wolff, J. (2024) (eds) *Structural Injustice and the Law*, London: UCL Press.

Martell, L. (2023) *Alternative Societies: For a Pluralist Socialism*, Bristol: Bristol University Press.

Marx, K. (2000) 'Critique of the Gotha Programme' in D. McLellan (ed) *Karl Marx: Selected Writings*, Oxford: Oxford University Press, pp.610–616.

Masiero, S. (2016) 'Digital Governance and the Reconstruction of the Indian Anti-poverty System' *Oxford Development Studies*, Vol.818, pp.1–16.

Mazzucato, M. (2014) *The Entrepreneurial State*, London, New York and Delhi: Anthem Press.

Mazzucato, M. (2016) 'Innovation, the State and Patient Capital' in M. Jacobs and M. Mazzucato (eds) *Rethinking Capitalism: Economics and Policy for Sustainable Growth*, Oxford: Wiley-Balckwell.

Mazzucato, M. (2018) *The Value of Everything*, London: Penguin.
Mazzucato, M. (2021) *Mission Economy: A Moonshot Guide to Changing Capitalism*, Milton Keynes: Allen Lane, Penguin.
Mazzucato, M. (2023) 'Concerning the Economics of the Common Good: From Correcting Market Failures to Shaping Collective Goals' *Journal of Economic Policy Reform*, Vol. 27, No.1, pp.1–24. Available at: www.tandfonline.com/doi/epdf/10.1080/17487870.2023.2280969?needAccess=true
McLellan, D. (1977) (ed) *Karl Marx Selected Writings*, Oxford: Oxford University Press.
Milanovic, B. (2022) 'Long Term: Difficulties of Import Substitution and Delocalization, GP Opinion', Available at: www.globalpolicyjournal.com/blog/16/03/2022/long-term-difficulties-import-substitution-and-delocalization (accessed 18 October 2022).
Miliband, R. (1970) 'The Capitalist State: Reply to Poulantzas' *New Left Review*, Vol.59, pp.53–60, reprinted in R. Blackburn (ed) *Ideology in Social Science*, London: Fontana.
Mill, J. (1937) *An Essay on Government*, Cambridge: Cambridge University Press.
Mingardi, A. (2015) 'A Critique of Mazzucato's Enterpreneurial State' *Cato Journal*, Vol.35, No.3, pp.603–625.
Mohamed, S., Png, M.-T. and Isaac, W. (2020) 'Decolonial AI: Decolonial Theory as Socio-technical Foresight in Artificial Intelligence' *Philosophy and Technology*, Vo.33, pp.659–684.
Moles, A. and Parr, T. (2019) 'Distributions and Relations: A Hybrid Account' *Political Studies*, Vol.67, No.1, pp.132–148.
Morgan, J. (2015) 'The Contemporary Relevance of a Cambridge Tradition: Economics as Political Economy, Political Economy as Social Theory and Ethical Theory' *Cambridge Journal of Economics*, Vol.40, No.2, pp.663–760.
Mueller, J. C. (2019) 'What Can Sociologists of Globalisation and Development Learn from Nicos Poulantzas?' *Progress in Development Studies*, Vol.19, No.14, pp.284–303.
Munyaradzi, M. and Mubaya, R. (2016) *African Philosophy and Thought Systems: A Search for a Culture and Philosophy of Belonging*, Langaa: ProQuest Ebook.
Murtinu, S. Foss, N. and Klein, P. G. (2022) 'The Entrepreneurial State: An Ownership Competence Perspective' in C. Wennberg and C. Sandström (eds) *Questioning the Entrepreneurial State: Status-Quo, Pitfalls and the Need for Credible Innovation Policy*, Cham: Springer.
Nabudere, D. W., and Simon, D. (2019) 'Julius Kambaragwe Nyerere (1922–1999)' in D. Simon (ed) *Key Thinkers on Development*, London and New York: Routledge.

Nelson, R. and Winter, S. (1982) *An Evolutionary Theory of Economic Change*, Cambridge, MA, and London: The Belnkap Press of Harvard University Press.

Noble, A. U. (2018) *Algorithms of Oppression: How Search Engines Reinforce Racism*, New York: New York University Press.

Nozick, R. (1974) *Anarchy State and Utopia*, Oxford: Blackwell.

Nussbaum, M. (2000) *Women and Human Development: The Capabilities Approach*, Cambridge: Cambridge University Press.

Nussbaum, M. (2006) *Frontiers of Justice: Disability, Nationality, Species Membership,* Cambridge, MA: Harvard University Press.

OECD (2012) *Innovation for Development.*

Offe, C. (1984) *Contradictions of the Welfare State*, London: Hutchinson.

Okolo, C. T., Aruleba, K. and Obaido, G. (2023) 'Responsible AI in Africa – Challenges and Opportunities' in D. Okaibedi Eke, K. Wakunuma and S. Akintoye (eds) *Responsible AI in Africa*, Leicester: Palgrave Macmillan, pp.1–12. https://link.springer.com/book/10.1007/978-3-031-08215-3

O'Neill, C. (2016) *Weapons of Maths Destruction: How Big Data Increases Inequality and Threatens Democracy,* New York: Crown Publishing Group.

Palma, G. (1978) 'Dependency: A Formal Theory of Underdevelopment or a Methodology for Analysis of Concrete Situations of Underdevelopment?' *World Development*, Vol.6, No.7/8, pp.881–1029.

PapaGreen, D. and Kirk, T. (2021) Agencies of Development in Development' in T. Allen and A. Thomas (eds) *Poverty and Development in the 21st Century*, 3rd Edition, Oxford: Oxford University Press, pp.76–102.

Papaioannou, T. (2012) *Reading Hayek in the 21st Century: A Critical Inquiry into His Political Thought*, London: Palgrave Macmillan.

Papaioannou, T. (2014) 'Innovation and Development in Search of a Political Theory of Justice' *International Journal of Technology and Globalisation*, Vol.7, No.3, pp.179–202.

Papaioannou, T. (2016) 'Sen and Marx on Incentives and Justice: Implications for Innovation and Development' *Progress in Development Studies*, Vol.16, No.4, pp.1–17.

Papaioannou, T. (2018) *Inclusive Innovation for Development: Meeting the Demands of Justice through Public Action*, London: Routledge.

Papaioannou, T. (2020) 'Reflections on the Entrepreneurial State, Innovation and Social Justice' *Journal of Evolutionary Political Economy*, Vol.1, No.2, pp.199–220.

Papaioannou, T. (2021) 'Creative States: Is State-Led Risk-Taking the Answer to Post-Covid-19 Recovery?' *RSA Journal*, Vol.5584, No.1, pp.30–35.

Papaioannou, T. and Srinivas, S. (2019) 'Innovation as a Political Process of Development: Are Neo-Schumpeterians Value Neutral?' *Innovation and Development,* Vol.9, No.1, pp.141–158.

Papaioannou, T., Yanacopulos, H. and Aksoy, Z. (2009) 'Global Justice: From Theory to Development Action' *Journal of International Development*, Vol.21, pp.805–818.

Perez, C. (2002) *Technological Revolutions and Financial Capital: The Dynamics of Bubbles and Golden Ages*, Cheltenham: Edward Elgar.

Perez, C. (2016) 'Capitalism, Technology and a Green Global Age: The Role of History in Helping to Shape the Future' in M. Jacobs and M. Mazzucato (eds) *Rethinking Capitalism: Economies and Policy for Sustainable Growth*, Oxford: Wiley-Blackwell.

Planes-Satorra, S. and Paunov, C. (2017) 'Inclusive Innovation Policies: Lessons from International Case Studies' OECD Science, Technology and Industry Working Papers, Paris: OECD Publishing, Available at: www.oecd.org/content/dam/oecd/en/publications/reports/2017/04/inclusive-innovation-policies_2cd59154/a09a3a5d-en.pdf

Potts, J. (2018) 'Governing the Innovation Commons' *Journal of Institutional Economics*, Vol.14, No.6, pp.1025–1047.

Poulantzas, N. (1973) *Political Power and Social Classes*, London: New Left Books.

Poulantzas, N. (1974) *Fascism and Dictatorship: The Third International and the Problem of Fascism*, London: New Left Books.

Poulantzas, N. (1975) *Classes in Contemporary Capitalism*, London: Left Books.

Poulantzas, N. (1976) 'The Capitalist State: A Reply to Miliband and Laclau' *New Left Review*, Vol.1, No.95, pp.63–71.

Poulantzas, N. (1978) *State, Power, Socialism*, London and New York: Verso.

Practical Action (2016) *Technology Justice: A Call to Action*, Rugby, UK: Practical Action Publishing, Available at: https://practicalactionpublishing.com/book/2155/technology-justice

Prebisch, R. (1950) *The Economic Development of Latin America and Its Principal Problems*, Lake Success, NY: United Nations.

Raphael, D. (2001) *Concepts of Justice*, Oxford: Oxford University Press.

Rawls, J. (1972) *A Theory of Justice*, Oxford: Oxford University Press.

Rawls, J. (1999) 'Social Unity and Primary Goods' in S. Freeman (ed) *John Rawls: Collected Papers*, Cambridge Massachusetts: Harvard University Press.

Rise, M. (2018) 'Human Rights and Artificial Intelligence: An Urgently Needed Agenda' *Carr Center for Human Rights Policy*, Harvard Kennedy School, Available at: https://carrcenter.hks.harvard.edu/files/cchr/files/humanrightsai_designed.pdf

Rist, G. (2002) *The History of Development: From Western Origin to Global Faith*. London: Zed.

Roche, C., Wall, P. J. and Lewes, D. (2023) 'Ethics and Diversity in Artificial Intelligence: Policies, Strategies and Initiatives' *AI and Ethics*, Vol.3, pp.1095–1115.

Rostow, W. W. (1960) *Stages of Economic Growth: A Non-Communist Manifesto*, Cambridge: Cambridge University Press.

Sachs, W. (1992, 2010) *The Development Dictionary: A Guide to Knowledge Power*, London: Zed Books.

Sandström, C. and Alm, C. (2022) 'Directionality in Innovation Policy and the Ongoing Failure of Green Deals: Evidence from Biogas, Bio-ethanol, and Fossil Free Steel' in C. Wennberg and C. Sandström (eds) *Questioning the Entrepreneurial State: Status-Quo, Pitfalls and the Need for Credible Innovation Policy*, Cham: Springer.

Santos, D. S. B. (2018) *The Cognitive Empire: The Coming of Age or Epistemologies of the South*, Durhan and London: Duke University Press.

Scanlon, T. (2018) *Why Does Inequality Matter?* Oxford: Oxford University Press.

Scanlon, T. M. (1982) 'Contractualism and Utilitarianism' in A. Sen and B. Williams (eds) *Utilitarianism and Beyond*, Cambridge: Cambridge University Press, pp.103–128.

Scheffler, S. (2005) 'Choice, Circumstance and the Value of Equality' *Politics, Philosophy and Economics*, Vol.4, pp.5–28.

Scheffler, S. (2015) 'The Practice of Equality' in C. Fourie, F. Schuppert and I. Walliman-Helmer (eds) *Social Equality: On What it Means to be Equals*, Oxford: Oxford University Press.

Schemmel, C. (2011) 'Why Relational Egalitarians Should Care About Distributions' *Social Theory and Practice*, Vol.37, No.3, pp.365–390.

Schot, J. and Steinmueller, E. (2018) 'Three Frames for Innovation Policy: R&D, Systems of Innovation and Transformative Change' *Research Policy*, Vol.47, No.9, pp.1554–1567.

Schot, J. and Steinmueller, W. E. (2016) 'Framing Innovation Policy for Transformative Change: Innovation Policy 3.0' Science Policy Research Unit (SPRU) Working Paper, Available at: www.johanschot.com/wp-content/uploads/2016/09/Framing-Innovation-Policy-for-Transformative-Change-Innovation-Policy-3.0-2016.pdf

Schumacher, E. F. (1973) *Small Is Beautiful: A Study of Economics as If People Mattered*, London: Blond and Briggs.

Schumacher, E. F. (1979) *Good Work*, London: Jonathan Cape.

Schumpeter, J. A. (1934) *The Theory of Economic Development*, New Brunswick and London: Transaction Publishers.

Schumpeter, J. A. (2010) *Capitalism, Socialism and Democracy*, London and New York: Routledge.

Seers, D. (1969, 1979) 'The Meaning of Development' in D. Lehmann (ed) *Development Theory: Four Critical Studies*, London: Frank Cass.

Sen, A. K. (1980) 'Equality of What?' in S. McMurrin (ed) *Tanner Lectures on Human Values*, Cambridge: Cambridge University Press.

Sen, A. K. (1999) *Development as Freedom*, Oxford: Oxford University Press.

Sen, A. K. (2009) *The Idea of Justice*, Cambridge MA: Belknap Press.

Singer, H. W. (1964) *International Development, Growth and Change*, New York: McCraw-Hill.
Skinner, Q. (1989) 'The State' in T, Ball, J. Farr and R. L. Hanson (eds) *Political Innovation and Conceptual Change*, Cambridge: Cambridge University Press.
Skocpol, T. (2008) 'Bringing the State Back In: Retrospect and Prospect' *Scandinavian Political Studies*, Vol.31, No.2, pp.109–124.
Smith, A. (1759/1976) *The Wealth of Nations*, Oxford: Clarendon Press.
Smith, A. (1759/2010) *The Theory of Moral Sentiments*, Oxford: Oxford University Press.
Smith, A. and Fressoli, M. (2021) 'Post-Automation' *Futures*, Vol.132, pp.1–13.
Smith, A. Fressoli, M., Abrol, D. Around, E. and Ely, A. (2017) *Grassroots Innovation Movements: Pathways to Sustainability*, London and New York: Routledge.
Smith, A. and Stirling, A. (2018) 'Innovation, Sustainability and Democracy: An Analysis of Grassroots Contribution' *Journal of Self-Governance and Management Economics*, Vol.6, No.1, pp.64–97.
Smith, A., Vob, J-P. and Grin, J. (2010) 'Innovation Studies and Sustainability Transitions: The Allure of the Multi-level Perspectives and Its Challenges' *Research Policy*, Vol.39, pp.435–448.
Srinivas, S. (2014) 'Demand and Innovation: Paths to Inclusive Development' in S. V. Ramani (ed) *Innovation in India: Combining Economic Growth with Inclusive Development*, Cambridge: Cambridge University Press, pp.78–104.
Sriskandarajah, D. (2024) *Power to the People: Use your Voice to Change the World*, London: Headline Press.
Stirling, A. (2024) 'Responsibility and the Hidden Politics of Directionality: Opening Up "Innovation Democracies" for Sustainability Transformations' *The Journal of Responsible Innovation*, Special Issue on 'Critiquing the Direction for Innovation – The Role of Justice and Exnovation' Vol.11, No.1, pp.1–31.
Sveiby, K. E., Gripenberg, P. and Segercrantz, B. (2012) (eds) *Challenging the Innovation Paradigm*, New York: Routledge, pp.15–36.
Takala, V. Nordbäck, E. and Toivonen, T. (2020) 'The Entrepreneurial (Welfare) State? Tackling Social Issues through Challenge Prizes' *UCL Institute for Innovation and Public Purpose, Working Papers Series* (IPP WP 2020–02), Available at: https://discovery.ucl.ac.uk/id/eprint/10195842/1/Takala_iipp-wp-2020-02_the-entrepreneurial-welfare-state_final.pdf
Taylor, L. (2017) 'What Is Data Justice? The Case for Connecting Digital Rights and Freedoms Globally' *Big Data and Society*, July–December, pp.1–14.
Thomas, A. (2021) 'Meanings and Views of Development' in T. Allen and A. Thomas (eds) *Poverty and Development in the 21st Century*, 3rd Edition, Oxford: Oxford University Press, pp.48–75.

Thomas, H., Becerra, L. and Garrido, S. (2017) 'Socio-technical Dynamics of Counter-Hegemony and Resistance' in B. Godin and D. Vinck (eds) *Critical Studies of Innovation: Alternative Approaches to the Pro-Innovation Bias*, Cheltenham: Edward Elgar, pp.182–200.

Thomas, H., Fressoli, M. and Becerra, L. (2012) 'Science and Technology Policy and Social Ex/Inclusion: Analysing Opportunities and Constraints in Brazil Argentina' *Science and Public Policy*, Vol.39, pp.579–591.

Turgot, A.-R. (1750/1973) *Turgot on Progress, Sociology and Economics: A Philosophical Rerview of Successive Advances of the Human Mind, on Universal History and Reflections on the Formation and the Distribution of Wealth*, Cambridge: Cambridge University Press.

UNCTAD (2021) *Annual Report: Reducing Inequality*, Available at: https://unctad.org/annual-report-2021

UNRISD (2022) *Crises of Inequality: Shifting Power for a New Eco-Social Contract*, Geneva: UNRISD, Available at: www.unrisd.org/en/library/publications/crises-of-inequality

Valentini, L. (2012) 'Ideal vs Non-ideal Theory: A Conceptual Map' *Philosophy Compass*, Vol.7, No.9, pp.654–664.

Volacu, A. (2018) 'Bridging Ideal and Non-Ideal Theory' *Political Studies*, Vol.66, No.4, pp.877–902.

Wade, R. (1990) *Governing the Market: Economic Theory and the Role of Government in East Asian Industrialisation*, Princeton: Princeton University Press.

Walsh, S. (2021) 'Marx, Subsumption and the Critique' *Organisation*, Vol.1–6, pp.1–16.

Weale, A. (1998) 'From Contracts to Pluralism' in P. Kelly (ed) *Impartiality, Neutrality and Justice*, Edinburgh: Edinburgh University Press, pp.35–43.

Wennberg, K. and Sandström, C. (2022) (eds) *Questioning the Entrepreneurial State: Status-Quo, Pitfalls and the Need for Credible Innovation Policy*, Cham: Springer.

Wield, D., Tait, J., Mittra, J. and Mastroeni, M. (2017) 'Conceptualising and Practicing Multiple Knowledge Interactions in the Life Sciences' *Technological Forecasting and Social Change*, Vol.116, pp.308–315.

Winner, L. (1989) *The Whale and the Reactor: A Search for Limits in an Age of High Technology*, Chicago: University of Chicago Press.

Wolff, J. (2006) 'Models of Distributive Justice' Available at: https://sas-space.sas.ac.uk/678/1/J_Wolff_Justice.pdf

Wolff, J. (2015) 'Social Equality, Relative Poverty and Marginalised Groups' WorldPress, Available at: https://view.officeapps.live.com/op/view.aspx?src=https%3A%2F%2Fjonathanwolff.wordpress.com%2Fwp-content%2Fuploads%2F2014%2F11%2Fwolff-social-equality-relative-poverty-and-marginalised-groups.docx&wdOrigin=BROWSELINK

World Bank (1997) *World Development Report: The State in a Changing World*, Washington DC: World Bank.

World Bank (2018) 'Annual Report' Available at: https://documents1.worldbank.org/curated/en/630671538158537244/pdf/The-World-Bank-Annual-Report-2018.pdf

World Bank (2019) *The Changing Nature of Work.* World Development Report, Available at: http://documents1.worldbank.org/curated/en/816281518818814423/pdf/2019-WDR-Report.pdf

World Health Organisation (2020) *Solidarity Call to Action,* Available at: www.who.int/initiatives/covid-19-technology-access-pool/solidarity-call-to-action

Worstall, T. (2013) 'The Intellectual Hole at the Heart of Mariana Mazzucato's Entrepreneurial State' *Forbes,* Available at: www .forbes.com/sites/timworstall/2013/12/15/the-intellectual-hole-at-the-heart-of-mariana-mazzucatos-entrepreneurial-state/

Wright, E. O. (2010) *Envisioning Real Utopias*, New York: Verso.

Wright, E. O. (2012) 'Transforming Capitalism through Real Utopias' *American Sociological Review*, Vol.78, No.1, pp.1–25.

Young, I. M. (1990) *Justice and the Politics of Difference*, Princeton, NJ: Princeton University Press.

Young, I. M. (2001) 'Activist Challenges to Deliberative Democracy' *Political Theory*, Vol.29, pp.670–690.

Young, I. M. (2011) *Responsibility for Justice*, Oxford: Oxford University Press.

Ypi, L. (2012) *Global Justice and Avant-Garde Political Agency*, Oxford: Oxford University Press.

Zehavi, A. and Breznitz, D. (2017) 'Distribution Sensitive Innovation Policies: Conceptualisation and Empirical Examples' *Research Policy*, Vol.46, pp.327–336.

Ziegler, R. (2015) 'Justice and Innovation: Towards Principles for Creating a Fair Space for Innovation' *Journal of Responsible Innovation*, Vol.2, No.2, pp.184–200.

Ziegler, R. (2020) *Innovation Ethics and Our Common Futures*, Cheltenham and Northampton, MA: Edward Elgar.

Index

For Product Safety Concerns and Information please contact our EU representative GPSR@taylorandfrancis.com
Taylor & Francis Verlag GmbH, Kaufingerstraße 24, 80331 München, Germany

www.ingramcontent.com/pod-product-compliance
Ingram Content Group UK Ltd.
Pitfield, Milton Keynes, MK11 3LW, UK
UKHW022156190926
475702UK00003B/64
* 9 7 8 1 0 4 1 0 9 8 4 6 1 *